THEY CALL ME
COACH

IF I CAN YOU CAN

STEPHON LEARY

THEY CALL ME **COACH**

Quantity sales special discounts are available on quantity purchases by corporations, associations, and others. For details, contact the publisher at the address above.

Orders by U.S. trade bookstores and wholesalers. Email info@BeyondPublishing.net

The Beyond Publishing Speakers Bureau can bring authors to your live event. For more information or to book an event contact the Beyond Publishing Speakers Bureau speak@BeyondPublishing.net

The Author can be reached directly at BeyondPublishing.net

Manufactured and printed in the United States of America distributed globally by BeyondPublishing.net

BEYOND
PUBLISHING

New York | Los Angeles | London | Sydney

ISBN: 978-1-952884-11-5

The journey of discovering your purpose in life can be filled with many challenges, but God is faithful through it all. This book is the story of a young man whose life was drastically changed, defying the odds of a talented, impoverished, inner-city kid with no direction, no structure, and no educational foundation after he meets Coach Dave Stallman one day in a gym. This most-unlikely encounter led to a Hall of Fame Basketball Player's Camp in Florida: the late great "Pistol" Pete Maravich. This experience would change the course of his life forever. That young man is a black kid who left the inner city for the suburbs to live with a white family, who raised and trained him to be the man he is today. This story of a coach, a trainer, a mentor, a teacher, a counselor, a businessman, an entrepreneur, an inventor, and an author, who defied the odds of being born to an abusive, alcoholic dad and a loving, hardworking, single mom who raised six boys and one girl. His journey was filled with many challenges, but had a destination of a purpose-filled life. This is a story that illustrates that love has no color, and the power of love can serve as a changing agent to our culture and society. Through this story, you will learn that the power of God can manifest itself in the life of anyone who is willing to submit to His will and be used by Him. The journey of success and greatness comes with a price, and although there are many peaks and valleys along the way, if you stay the course and never give up or give in, God will see you through.

I want to thank some of the most important people in the world to me. First, I thank my God, My Lord, and My Savior, Jesus Christ, for saving me, setting my foot on a path to be able to have accomplished all that I have. Lord, thank you for leading me to write this book to share the love, faithfulness, mercy, goodness, grace, and the power of a loving God.

I want to thank my mom, Gladys Coleman, who endured great hardships to put me in the position I was in when my life drastically changed. A single mother of seven, my mom is one of the strongest and hardest-working people I know. Thank you for demonstrating those characteristics before me. Thank you, Mom, for your sacrifice and support of me to be the man I am today. Your protection of my gifts has kept me from going off course and choosing to make bad decisions. Thank you for sharing me with those who could help see that my gifts would make me a successful person. I want you to know, whatever we had was enough, because of your hard work and commitment to provide for your kids. Thank you, and I love you dearly.

There is not enough room, nor words, to express the gratitude I have in my heart, soul, and mind for Dave and Lynne Johnson. Dave and Lynne took me in as a 17-year-old kid and gave me a whole new outlook on life. One filled with knowledge, wisdom, and understanding of the love of God and His purpose for my life. But most of all, you loved me from the very first day I walked into your home, and you treated me like I was your very own. These two individuals were quick to obey God against all odds to bring an inner-city black kid to a predominantly white suburb and treat him as one of their very own children. The love and support you have shown me over the past 33 years will never be forgotten or go unnoticed. Thank you so much for giving me a second chance at life and for encouraging me on my journey to discover God's purpose for my life. Dad, thanks for setting a Godly example of a true man of God. One who loves God, his family, his church, and works hard every day to provide. Mom, thanks for *your sensitive spirit to the things of God, you have imparted so much love and wisdom while nurturing me as a young man and helping me become the man I am today. More importantly, you taught me to love praise and worship for God, which is something I use every day to bring peace and the presence of God into my life. I'm forever grateful!! I Love You More Than Words Can Express!*

A tribute to my siblings: the struggle was real, but we serve a faithful, loving, and mighty God. It wasn't always easy growing up, moving from one part of the city to the other, many times not having food or enough clothes, but we are all still here. God has a purpose and plan.

In order of oldest to youngest:

Willie Leary, his wife—Liza—and my nieces and nephew—Anthony, Chauntel, Elliz, and Angel: as a big brother, Willie took the time to take me everywhere to play pick-up basketball all over the city of Houston. He also took me in and supported me on my journey to be the best athlete I could be. Love you all!

Johnny Leary and my nieces and nephews, Latessa Robinson, Lakeisha Clark, Natassijia Washington, Kimico Washington, Darwyn Washington, and Derrick Spencer—my favorite pastor in the world: I am extremely proud of you for turning your life around and sowing seeds into the Kingdom. I love all the road trips we take and all the times you have tried to hook me up. When all else failed, Johnny provided the best entertainment for the family and served as a pastor in our hometown of Bunkie and Alexandria, Louisiana, sharing the message of Jesus Christ. You may never know the spiritual impact you made on our hometown and our spiritual heritage until God reveals it, but for now: well done. Love you all!

Stephanie Leary and my nephews, Gerald and Terrence— my sister is one of the most caring people I know. My hope and desire is that you will truly allow God to use the gifts He's giving you. You can make a difference in this world. Love you all!

Wallace Leary and sons, Chris Wallace, Jr. and Dwayne: I admire your independence and drive to be successful, and all the hard work you do to take care of your family. Although I never get to see you and your family, I think of you often. Love you all!

Bryan Leary, the hardest working man in show business, as they say. Bryan is a very loyal and loving person, who works hard at everything he does. Keep chasing those dreams. Love you, bro!

Jessie Coleman and son—Jessie Jr.—and his new baby girl: the baby of the bunch who loves family and all his siblings more than we knew. I appreciate your genuine desire to be used by God. Keep doing the right thing: God has a plan for you. Love you all!

Jackie Coleman and husband, Carson Daniels, Brandon, Ariana, and Takeya Coleman and family daughters—Taniah, Tianna, and Tailyn— my cousins who basically became my siblings. Thank you for always supporting me and believing in me. Specifically, to Jackie who has become my administrative assistant and personal assistant for my business. Also, for the spiritual encouragement, and dream interpretations of encouraging me to stay the course. Love all you guys!

Russell Coleman, who became like a little brother, but was a first cousin. You always make for great times at family functions. Keep working hard to accomplish your goals. Love you, my man!

Now, for my adopted siblings:

Jacob and Lynnette Johnson and kids, Luke and Joseph, I like to think of Jacob as the righteous one. His sincerity, genuine love, and commitment to God, his family, his friends, his wife, and his kids inspire me. Thank you for embracing me into the family as your brother. You were the firstborn of Mom and Dad; I imagine it wasn't easy to allow someone like me to come in and be the oldest. Thank you for your belief in me and always encouraging me that I could do it. Lastly, thanks for becoming my new editor. Love you, my brother, and I am looking forward to writing a book with you someday. Keep up the good work!

Scott Johnson was adopted just as I was, so we shared a common bond to know and discover our true person in life. Although we were met with many challenges, you are an inspiration for how far you have come. God has a purpose and plan for your life; I hope you find it and walk in it. Love you, bro!

Jessica Johnson Sloan, husband Jason, and daughters Stori, Micah, Lyric, and my little angel, Piper. Jessica demonstrated to me what true love is. My first night in the house, a little nine-year-old jumped in my bed and kissed me on the cheek and told me, "Good night, I love you." –even though I had not known her for more than a week. Still today, when I see her now in her thirties, she kisses me and tells me she loves me. This was the first time in my life I experience what true, Godly love was. A life-changing experience! I will forever love you! Love my nieces, who remind me so much of you in how they love Uncle Steph.

Billy Johnson— one of the most talented kids I have ever seen. Anything Billy put his mind to do, he was good at. Having you look up to me made me want to do what was right growing up. Billy was also adopted and is the biological brother of Scott. May you rest in peace, my dear brother. I miss you!

Special thanks and loving tribute to the Freeman family, a second home growing up in inner-city Houston. My late "other mother"—Betty Anne Freeman—who battled cancer, and unfortunately, was called home by God. Mom, you will always mean the world to me. I miss your smile and your hugs. I will never forget how, whenever I entered your presence, you would always say, "Boy, you better come over here and give Momma a hug." You will never know how much that meant to me. Thank you so much for helping me through the struggle. Those many times I came over to eat when we didn't have food, not even cereal or a sandwich. I will forever cherish the many Sundays we spent watching football with you, and the boys. You planted a seed of love in me that will never go away. I miss you so much to this day, and I love you. My brothers from my other mother, Dale, and his family, Albert, with his lovely wife, my sister—Nikki—my goddaughters—Nina and Dee—Brian and his family, and Duane and his family: thanks for being my second family, and giving me all the love and support through our 43 years of family-ship. Albert Freeman and I became the best friends. We were in the same grade and class in elementary. We are still the best of friends, and brothers, today.

Special thanks to Grandma Opal Berard, Aunt Michelle Berard and family, Doug Berard and family: words cannot express my gratitude and appreciation for how you accepted me into the Johnson family. From day one, you saw the good in me, believed in me, and encouraged me to be who I am today. Grandma will always be my sports girl. The connection we had from day one laid the foundation for you to pour out your love upon me. I love you. Aunt Michele, I will never forget these words, "Steph, come with us; I'll buy you something." Like mom, you were my shopping buddy, you helped me learn how to dress, and you were always full of positivity and belief in me about who I could become. Love you!

Uncle Doug and family, you're the man. The countless conversations over sports were priceless, and your kind words and generosity will never be forgotten. Love you, my man!

In tribute to my late Grandma Joan Ketchmark, you accepted me into the Johnson family. Your quiet temperament was golden. Love you!

Uncle Paul Johnson, although you were quiet, the many small conversations we had were very enlightening and profitable. Love the times we laughed and told stories. Love you!

To all my former students, players, campers, and trainees— you gave me the platform to learn and grow into the man I came to be. I thank you for all of your hard work with that level of commitment to my purpose. I am forever grateful.

To my Shooting Stars coaches and staff, thank you for your belief in my vision for the organization. Just know, your hard work and your dedication and commitment has not gone unnoticed. Thank you for your desire to share in the lives of young people and help them become all they are capable of being. I respect you, and I appreciate you for all the long days and hours together. You are my forever brothers and sisters. Love you all!

To Albert and Nikki Freeman and family. Albert is still my longest standing best friend. We met at the early age of eight years old by being in the same classroom together. We were living a couple doors down from each other, and we have remained friends until now. Through all the ups and downs, twist and turns, and distance in between us, nothing could keep us apart.

Your friendship and brotherhood has meant everything to me over the years. I love you forever, my brother. Nikki is the best cook from scratch I've ever known. You know I love you, girl.

Dale Freeman, this friendship was established between our families and Albert and my older brother, Willie. We had so much fun at the courts, talking hoops and sports together. What awesome times, my brother. I always admired your basketball abilities. They inspired me. Love you, man!

Brian Freeman, you were always one of the most talented and competitive people. The most important thing about you is how you love and support your friends and family, as well as all the time you spent playing football and basketball, watching sports, playing cards, and competing. Everything we did was the best time of my life. Love you, bro.

Baby bro, Duane Freeman, I have always enjoyed your attention to the world around, your intellect, and your drive to be successful. Love you!

Special thanks to my Faith West Foundation— my first coach job to Vicki Callender. Abster and Hannah, thank you for your devotion to Christ. Your devotion to loving people the way God does and always seeing the good in everyone. Your friendship was priceless. All the times of encouragement, love, and prayers we shared. Thank you for believing in me. Rest in heaven to your wonderful husband, Mike Callender, who was an unbelievable man, husband, and father.

The Galbraith family—Mike Kendra and Ryan—Sally, my Team Mom, and my bus driver— your sweet, kind, and loving spirit was priceless. You were not just a team mom or bus driver your loving way of bringing peace and unity was immeasurable thank you so much for all your support.

And to Bill and Leenie Gavulic, as well as Lauren and Lyndsey, who became the bus driver for Handy Man and did everything else we needed. Leenie your passion and fireball spirit was awesome. Thank you so much for your support and all your hard work to make my sports teams successful.

The Geloneck family, Jeff and Teresa, thank you for making my job easier with all the pictures, planning, and snacks you provided and the monetary support to help us build championship programs.

The Herndon family and Nick: Thanks, Val and Wes, for your support and fighting for us to build competitive programs.

Tony and Shelly Patterson and Josh: To Shelly, I would say we were one of the few schools who had an athletic trainer, and thank you for your belief in me and my vision.

The Self family, Shannon and Chad, thanks for your support, and partnering with me on building a solid foundation.

The Lakey Family Shane thanks for all your support and hardwork.

The Powers Family Bill and Beth thanks for all your support and hardwork.

The Walker Family Russell and Ryan thanks for all your support and hardwork.

The Dickey Family Avery-Lynn Seth and Meredith thanks for all your support and hardwork.

The Davis/Nemeth/Armstrong Family Leslian (John Edward and Betty Ann RIH My Friends I Miss You), Hunter Kailee, Elizabeth Thank you for your support.

As an athletic director and coach at such a young age, I want to thank all my coaches at Faith West and all my colleagues for embracing my leadership and allowing me to build a great private school program with many championships.

Special thanks to these families who became more than just participants in the Shooting Stars program; you were the foundational pieces who became pillars. Thank you for your hard work and commitment: the Smiths (Felicia and Jourdan Sr. Jourdan, Jacob, Shaun), the Hughes (Coach T and Fradreaka, Torrence, Vonte), the Hynes (Gerald and Cousin Twyla Chris, Brianna, Kenedy), the McClurgs (Susan and Tom, Ryan, Jackson), the Geddes (Dan and Missy, Dane, Daelyn, Gage "Run Gage Run", Andie), the Welches (Rhonda, Chance), the Burnetts (Mark and Jessie Jake, Anna), the Sjolunds (Kristian, Jonas), the Webers (Bob and Siobhan, Jack and Thomas), the Bulawas (Brett and Dustine Drew, Bayli), the Fontenots (Teno and April, Tena and Cam), and the Selvages (my brother Shaun and family Zadi, Zack, Kevin, Zoë, and Khalil). For my girls' program Morrows (Alex) and Moonsammys (Duane and Marbella Claudia, Vanessa), the Wheelers (Robin, Jessica, Kyle), the Kaliseks (Dan and Leianne, Kayla, Kade), Lynne and Maddie Bittle, and the Lopezes (Mike and Shari, Mikaela), thank you for your commitment from day one until the end AAU.

Thank you to the Moonsammy family—Duane, Vanessa, and my little Claudia—for always being there, and for Marbella for the photoshoot for me.

Thank you to Felecia Smith and family; thank you for your service to the program and helping us build a solid foundation and launching the website. Thank you for all of your hard work and dedication through the years.

Thank you, Jourdan Sr., for your support and commitment to the program.

Thank you, Terrence and Fradreaka Hughes, for all your hard work and coaching. I always could depend on you.

Thanks, Dreak, for your commitment and support.

Thanks to Gerald and Twyla Hynes for spending all that extra time teaching and instructing the game, like it should be. And my main man, Chris, for going from player to coach to administrator. One of the brightest minds in basketball, and thanks for helping with social media and the website.

To the Sjolund family—Becky and Bjorn—for your support and belief in me to develop your boys to be the best players they were capable of being and offering your home as a place to train to continue to develop young people. I appreciate your love and your support. You will always be family to me.

Thank you, Markus, for your drawings and artistry.

Special thanks to Dave and Gail Stallman. Dave was the coach who found me in the Memorial High School gym, and invited me to attend the Pistol Pete Maravich Basketball Camp in Clearwater, Florida. Later, he was responsible for why I left home to attend Houston Christian Prep, now Faith West Academy in Katy. This is the place where I began my journey as a Christian. His wife, Gail, is the sweetest, most loving, and caring person. She treated me like the son she never had. Also, their wonderful daughters, Charity and Rachel, who loved and accepted me like a brother.

Thank you to the late, great "Pistol" Pete Maravich and his late father, Press Maravich. Pistol Pete Maravich taught me the most valuable lesson a young man of my age and stature could learn. He taught me the value of character and positive attitude and believing in others. The things you *taught me, I shall never forget, and everything I do, I will always remember to value my teammates and to live a life of character over talent. You were the first to believe in my ability to become a great player. You instilled in me the ability to train and teach others the game of basketball, and most of all "It's your character that counts". Thank you for giving me to the Lord—I am a life that was changed. You are forever in my heart and memory.*

Special thanks to Faith West Pastor Bill Patterson and Gary Kerr for allowing me to attend Faith West as a senior and earn a scholarship to play basketball at Liberty University. My diploma was the first and only high school diploma in my immediate family.

Mr. Patterson, thank you for allowing the team to have such an awesome year. Your hard work and dedication didn't go unnoticed.

Also Special Thanks to Gary and Lori Kerr as part of Faith West experience, Gary Kerr was instrumental in my success as a faith West student and along with my principal, Rick Tankersley, these two later hired me in my first coaching job and believed enough in me to appoint me as athletic director and trust me to build a great program. Thank you Rick and Sharon Tankersley for believing in me and seeing God's gifts in me. Rick I will never forget that Sunday after church when you asked me to coach and teach at Faith West. Forever Grateful!

My first youth pastor, Jim Stanka and family (Josh, John, and Julia) who taught me wisdom and integrity and gave me a sense of direction in life. He also believed in me and supported me to become the man I am today. Allen and Mary Strickland were the assistant youth pastors and my favorite teachers. Mary inspired a young man with a difficult learning background to strive to be the best academic student I was capable of being.

To Brad Morgan and Ann Marie, my high school chaplain: Brad's passion and love for God still inspires me today! Thank you for being a mentor and friend.

To Mike Gifford, who was a baseball coach and later on my staff at Faith West. Thank you for your kindness and support and for always believing in me.

Also, special thanks to all my former students and players from Faith West, Cypress Christian, Liberty University, Palm Beach Atlantic University, and Texas A&M International University. My former players still remain in a group chat that gives me so much laughter and great conversations—Derek Barnes, Sean tucker, Spencer Foreman, Matthew Smith, Chris Swan, Ignacio Garcia, Tracy Johnson, and Jerante Morgan.

To My original Reaching New Heights Basketball Training and Camps, Shot Callers AAU, Chris Connolly and family brother Paul and Dave and parents, Andrew Lasker proud of the man and basketball player you became) Martin Davis, and My whole Shooting Stars Organization, you have been instrumental in my journey to shaping and molding me into being a successful coach, teacher, and trainer.

Special thanks to all my high school and college teammates—especially to my Houston Christian Prep team: you accepted me from day one, an inner-city black kid who was new to the school and somewhat shell-shocked in this new environment. You guys made me feel right at home. Although we fell short in the state championship game, we made history together by winning the NACA National Championship, but more than that, you became my brothers through Coach Stallman's leadership. The many road trips and long drives established a bond in my life I had never experienced before. The Coach Stallman sing-alongs were the best. My life was forever changed through that one year with you guys. I will forever be grateful to you and love you guys. To Anthony and Terry Boling, Billy Honeck, and Reed Runnels, who have all remained dear friends of mine today, I appreciate you for being there for me.

To my Liberty teammates, thank you for being a part of my journey. I had the best time in college and will always cherish the bond we built in the dorms, in practices, road trips, and especially the games. We were the first NCAA Division One Basketball Team for Liberty University— now look at it. We endured a lot at LU, trailblazing for the next generation, and through all the ups and downs and many challenges we made it. I will forever be grateful for our friendships, many of you who are still brothers and friends today. Zach Harris, my white chocolate brother from another mother, you're my man. Bro, you were a friend from the first day we met and came in as freshmen, and we remain friends and brothers, even now. No matter what discrimination we faced, I always knew Zach was on my side. I especially appreciate your friendship and brotherhood—even now, during this time of racial unrest. Love you, my brother.

Chris Toomer, my chocolate brother from another mother, I love your drive and determination, and your sincere support of me. You mean a great deal to me, bro, and always will.

Other teammates—Paul Nazigan, Matt Hildebrand, Danny Curbinson, Darius Hunter, Daryl Williams, Brett Badget, Brett Anthony, Jody Chapman, Tim Scarbourough, Julius Nwosu—have all remained close friends. I appreciate our group chat.

To my extended Liberty family, you know who you are, the football players, and other athletic teams, I'm eternally grateful for you and your friendships. We came together like brothers at a time when we felt outnumbered or uncomfortable. We made LU a great experience. I will cherish all the competitive video games, cards, hanging out, haircuts, and holding down "The Wall in Demoss".

Special shoutout to James McKnight— although you were on the football team, we built a bond that still lasts today. I appreciate and love you, my brother. Proud of the work you're doing; keep serving and honoring God.

Special thanks to Liberty University and the late, great Jerry Falwell, the founder and president of Liberty University, who made a lasting impact on my life. I credit him for imparting visions and dreams into my life and believing I can achieve greatness through a committed relationship with my Lord and Savior, Jesus Christ. Dr. Jerry Falwell also made a call to Dr. David Clark at Palm Beach Atlantic University and gave me a wonderful reference to become a head coach. To Jeff Meyer and family—who gave me a scholarship to play basketball and an opportunity to earn the first and only college degree in my family. Coach Meyer made me a student assistant coach my senior year when I was injured. Jeff Meyer still today remains a close mentor and friend and encourages me in all my endeavors.

Thank you to Coach Rick Burby, Ken Brooks, Greg McCauley Randy Dunton and Families my assistant Coaches as a college player. Thank you to Rick Burby for finding me in a gym in Tennessee and recruiting me to Liberty. Thank you for demanding excellence out of me and hard work.

Also, thanks to my Liberty University professors and administration for making me the man I am today: "A Champion for Christ", which is the university model. Also, thanks to Liberty for giving me my second coaching job.

To Randy Dunton and Kim Graham, who hired me as my first college coaching job. To Athletic Director Robert White and President Dr. David Clark of Palm Beach Atlantic University, who gave me my first opportunity to be a head coach at the college level. To Dr. Debbie Snell and Dr. Ray Keck, who gave me my second opportunity to be a head coach at the college level.

My special friend who helped me along the way and remained my friend and brother until now, Demaris Rayaka Dray—my college roommate who joined me in Houston to build my first athletic program, and remains a major part of my Reaching New Heights Organization today. Demaris and I spent many nights discussing the future and building something to impact young people through education and athletics. You're my main man, my brother. Thanks for all the good talk and time we spent together.

To Tim Scarborough, my first college roommate who encouraged me and believed in me to be a great player. Thanks for all the trips to Philly and introducing me to the Philly steak and cheese subs. Thanks for being my first college roommate and making our little dorm room a place to dream and enjoy college and inspire one another to be great. I'm so proud to see you living out your dream as a basketball analyst while building a wonderful family. Julius Nwosu "My Boy", I will never forget Coach Meyer bringing you to my room that night. It was the first of many wonderful moments. Your journey and the man you are inspires me. Julius was another college roommate who continued to believe in me and be a brother to me. I love and appreciate you, Big Fella. Nothing but great things to come for you.

Rod Watson, wife Laura, and daughters Renecia, Halana, and Fatima: you were my first pupil. I'm so proud of the man you have become and the success you have experienced.

Dawn Shuler—my best girl friend who always pushed me and stood by me through all my ups and downs—Lynn Cummins and family, Sheriee Harrelson and family—my personal assistants who help me focus on being a good coach, and was the best mom assistant a person could ask for—and Shelly Patterson—my sister in Christ, who always believed in me as a coach and mentor—I'm honored to be your son's godfather. Thank you for all the prayers and encouragement.

To Jared Goodwin and Trey Austin, I want to personally say thank you for believing in me. Jared, you were my first hire as an assistant coach. Your friendship and brotherly love have been immensely appreciated over the years. We met while you were a manger and student, and we have continued our friendship until today. I love and appreciate you, my man. Trey, I had the opportunity to watch you blossom from a high school player into a great, young coach. It has been a pleasure to share in all your experiences. I'm extremely proud of you and all your accomplishments. Keep up the good work.

To all my nieces, nephews, aunts, uncles, and cousins who always encouraged me and believed in me!

A big thank you to all my former players and parents in high school and college for believing in me and giving me 100 percent in practice and games. Also, thank you for allowing me to teach and train you through life principles, Christian characters, and competitive drills.

Lastly, to my prize possessions, my children: Katacha Miller—my goddaughter, who is the sweetest woman I know. I'm extremely proud of the woman and teacher you have become; Josh Patterson—my godson who aspires to be a coach as well and has coached with me the last several years—keep up the good work, don't give up on your dreams; Renecia Watson, daughter of Rod Watson, chase your dreams and achieve them. To my godson, Justin Steven Barnes, and my former player, Derek Barnes, who believed in me to aspire to have me as his first child's godfather. I love you, and Justin, I will always be here to help you accomplish your goals and dreams.

To my goddaughter, Tailyn Baker, you remind me so much of your mother. I will always be here for you, and I love you. My goddaughters, Nina and Dee Freeman, daughters of my childhood best friend Albert Freeman, I am so proud of the women you have become. You exude love and passion and reflect the love of Christ, and I'm thankful to see that in you, too. I love you!

London Williams, my one and only daughter, who is my heart and soul, I love you soooo much. You make Daddy proud to be in your life. I remember holding you as a baby and putting you to sleep like it was yesterday. I am very proud of the young lady you are becoming. I'm honored to be called your daddy. You are my true princess!

Julien Williams, my son, my little man: I tried to make you a baller, but you weren't having any of that. You are gifted in so many ways. Keep working hard, because whatever you choose to do, I know you will be successful. I'm very proud of you, as well. I pray you will continue to be the sweet, wonderful young man you are. I love you dearly, my son!

To anyone I may have missed, thank you for your love and support over the years!

TABLE OF CONTENTS

1

THE EARLY YEARS

The year of 1968, in a hospital in Pineville, Louisiana, a son was born to Gladys Marie Coleman and Willie Leary. This was the beginning of the journey of an infant named Stephone Leary, also known as Stephon.

That child was me. I was the fifth child of seven children in a household that only had two bedrooms. The house was not in the best of shape, but it was a house, nonetheless. Born to an alcoholic and abusive father was a great challenge, but it provided the greatest escape in my life. Due to gambling, physical and emotional abuse, and alcoholism, when I was a five-year-old, I went to sleep in a bed in Bunkie, Louisiana, and woke up in Houston, Texas. At sunrise the next morning, I walked out the door to go outside, and with great fear, I screamed and asked my mom where we were. My mom sat us down as kids and told us she had left my dad in Louisiana, and we were starting a new life in Houston.

As a kid, I grew up a very shy, quiet, and fearful child! Houston was a very big city, and it was difficult to be accepted into the neighborhoods. I recall moving so many times, I lost count. We lived all over the city, and it seemed as if each neighborhood we moved to, the worse the situation was. My mother worked two to three jobs to clothe and feed us, but sooner than later, her absence began to take its toll on me and my siblings. We basically grew up not parented, because my mother was never home. Even if she got a break from work, she started going out and having a good time herself. This behavior had a major effect on the development of my siblings and me! However, as I look back, what else should a 30-year-old woman be doing? For that reason, I don't find fault with my mom; it was just unfortunate that she was a 30-year-old with seven kids.

As each year passed, our struggles and difficulties worsened. My siblings and I first began to fight for our respect and acceptance into the hood, trying our best not to give into gang violence or get beaten up every day. Each passing month, the pressure got even stronger, and we also struggled with going to school to get an education, because there was no one home to make sure we went to school. My mom worked as a cafeteria cook, and later the supervisor, so she always had to leave the house early—before we woke up. All I can remember from when I was a kid was my mom coming in the room and saying, "Y'all need to get up and go to school, and if you want breakfast, you'll have to eat at school." This became a decision at a very early age: whether or not we wanted to be educated. Unfortunately, this decision is one inner-city low-income families have to make far too often. This choice to sleep in or go to school is why many in the inner-city are not educated. Single moms having to run out the door for work, while children are made to get up, get dressed, and walk to school. You also had to deal with the outside pressures of the hood. As a youngster, I became scared to go to school, because of my fear of failure. I might get beat up on the way to and from school, or have to fight to fend for myself and my hood.

Coming from a small town in Louisiana, we didn't have these pressures. The hood life was introduced to us as we relocated to Houston. So, at a very young age, you learn fight and run. It wasn't long before you learn that growing up in the hood or inner city was about deciding to be educated, fighting to belong, and surviving. Yet, a good thing about the hood was the competition.

2

FIGHTING BACK

There was one particular day when my brothers and I were walking home, and a group of guys attempted to pick on us. But this time, we did not run home. My older brothers and I were tired of running, so we fought back that day, and miraculously, we were never picked on again. I believe this was one of my first lessons in my life: we must protect and defend ourselves. This life principle is one of the most valued principles we can learn—protect and defend. Looking back as a mature Christian, Scripture tells us we don't **fight** against flesh and blood, but against powers, against principalities, against spiritual wickedness in high places (Ephesians 6:12). Scripture also tell us to put on the full armor of God, so we can take our stand against the devil's schemes (Ephesians 6:11). You see, as a child, I learned to take a stand and fight, so when I became a Christian, these were principles I could easily understand and embrace. You must understand, there is an enemy who does not want you to find your purpose in this life.

Well, as soon as we got comfortable where we were, it was time to move again. Fortunately, this move was a good move. We moved from fifth ward Houston to the third ward of Houston. This move became one of God's greatest blessings in my life. We changed schools to Turner Elementary.

This is the school where I began to love school. Also, we moved next door to the Freeman family, who had four boys—Dale, Albert, Brian, and Duane—with a wonderful mother, Betty Freeman. She became a second mom, and Albert Freeman was the same age as I was, and we were in the same classroom. We walked to school together and played together after school, along with all our siblings. We became family, we stayed over each other's houses all the time, we ate at each other's houses, and our moms supervised us when our own mothers were not around. This was a great time in my life.

When my older siblings became teens, life came unraveled. My siblings began to drop out of school to work, and we lived what most people call the "hustle life", or surviving the hood. We did whatever it took to get some money to buy food and clothes, because we were a less fortunate, welfare family, even though my mom worked two jobs. The welfare system of assistance was a tremendous benefit, but in most cases, still not enough. Food stamps and assistance was just another way to make many families struggle more. The more kids you have, the more assistance you get, and unfortunately, our inner-city communities have families who simply depend on the welfare program as a way of life. If you get a job and report a certain amount of money as your income, your assistance would be cut. So, families have to choose to work and accept what little assistance they can get or remain on the welfare program to survive. This is the problem that plagues communities still today. We need to revamp the welfare system to where it actually makes parents more responsible. We need more resources and outlets to facilitate families like the one I grew up in, where a mom was working two jobs and on welfare, so she could parent and supervise her kids. Far too many kids are having to make a tough choice to work or be educated, and parents who have or need the assistance of the government to make it.

3

BLESSED BY THE UNKNOWN

While my siblings began to live that life, I became very interested in sports, and began to join the YMCA athletic teams and other community organizational teams. This became a life saver for me and launched me toward my purpose in life. It also provided an incentive for me to go to school and do well. Before my involvement in sports, I went to school for two reasons: to eat for free and recess. As I began to attend school regularly, my teacher took notice, and began to get involved in my education. From grades three to five, I was truly blessed by my teachers in ways I didn't yet understand. At this time in my life, I had no knowledge of Jesus dying on the Cross for my sins in order to give me a new, eternal life. My elementary teachers made such an impact on my life, and I am eternally grateful for them still today. Mrs. Howelton, Mr. Thompson, and Mrs. Smith probably didn't realize they saved my life and helped set me on the path to fulfilling my purpose. There were many times over those years my teachers helped me get a haircut, fed me after school, gave me a ride home, and encouraged me to stay in school and get an education. My teachers throughout elementary extended special grace to me after learning of my living situation; I was truly blessed during this time in my life. As one could imagine, my love for sports grew immensely. I didn't realize that there was a fee to compete on these teams, yet somehow, my fees were always taken care of. I was also blessed to always get a coach who inspired me and believed in me.

4

THE BLESSING AND THE CURSE

As we seek to discover our purpose in this life, we must pay close attention not to allow our God-given gifts to supersede the giver of our gifts. While I was playing football, baseball, basketball, and track, I began to gain confidence in myself and desired to be a professional athlete in football, baseball, or basketball. Each coach I had as a youth continually spoke positive, encouraging words to me about staying in school, staying out of trouble, not getting involved in drugs or alcohol, and not committing a crime. As I remember today, I had no real reason for why I did not make the same decisions my friends and siblings seemed to be making at the time. It was as if I had found my true calling in life—to be a professional athlete. Even though I played every sport imaginable year-round, my mother was not able to attend any of my games. However, she encouraged me to keep doing well, and one day, I would make it.

Because I was so successful at a young age, I can look back and see the curse my talent had on me. The real reason for my making positive decisions had everything to do with sports, not because of my purpose, my destiny, or honoring my gift giver. Little did I know, I was not preparing myself for that day when I could no longer play sports. What would I do? How would I act? What would you do? I guess it depends on who you are. The ability to get up, look up, and move on has everything to do with the depth of your character and foundation in your beliefs. You have heard it said, "only the strong can survive." For my experience, it is the strength of who you are!

Sports saved my life, which was a blessing, but the curse was that I became so driven to be successful that sports, it's all I did. I think there were many things I could have learned along the way in my life, had I not been so involved in every sport. This also meant that in the summers, when my mom and siblings would travel back to visit relatives and my dad, I was oftentimes not available to go, because I was playing a sport. One of the most impactful things that happened in my life was when I did get an opportunity to go back to my hometown of Bunkie and see my relatives and my dad. I showed up with the rest of my siblings to visit my dad, and as kids, we always asked for money to buy something to snack on or take money back to Houston. This particular time, my dad gave everyone money, except for me, because I did not come to visit him enough, because I was so in love with my sports. This was very difficult and devastating for me to hear. However, in a strange way, it made me more determined to be successful, so then, I would never have to rely on asking my dad for money. With my mom struggling to make ends meet, and my dad not wanting to help me, I begin to gamble to earn money. In some strange way, I thought I had a gift of gambling or God blessed me to gamble, because most often, I won, and I used that money to buy myself food when there was none at home, and also to buy clothes and shoes my mom could not afford. For the most part, I was a really good kid who made good decisions in my life. However, the one decision that almost cost me my ability to be successful in sports was stealing. Because I played sports, when I got home, all the food was already gone, so for some strange reason, I came up with the idea to go into the grocery store, fill up the brown bags with whatever snacks I wanted, take it up front, and ask the cashier to watch my groceries while I went to the restroom. I would come out of the restroom, grab the bag, and walk out the door and head home, where I hid my snacks in the closet or in a place where no one else could find them. I repeated this action a few times, before one day, when I filled the bags with groceries, a manager came up to me as I was walking out and said, "I did not see you pay for those groceries. Whose groceries are those?" I looked at the manager and lied that they were my mom's. The manager said, "I did not see a woman walk in the store with you. Are you telling me the truth?"

I said, "Yes, sir, I am."

As I proceeded to walk out the door, the manager told me, "I'm pretty sure I did not see you, nor your mom, pay for those groceries. I know something's not right. Therefore, I'm going to let you go this time, but I better not catch you back in the store without an adult buying those groceries." That was the last time I ever stole anything in my life.

Living in the inner city and being raised by a single mom was challenging. Many times, as kids, we tried to find things to do to make money. My brothers got involved with delivering newspapers. That lasted for a little while, but it was not sustainable. I had a really good friend who played football with me, who tried to introduce me to being a delivery boy for drug dealers. This seemed like a good idea for a young boy to earn some money. However, I also knew it was dangerous, because of the violence surrounding the drugs and drug dealer. I can recall one of my best friends, who was probably the best player on my little league football team and was the quarterback while I was the wide receiver, and he choose to make deliveries for drug dealers. One day, while coming home from the park, I saw an ambulance up the sidewalk from where we lived, and as I came around the corner, I saw my friend's mom crying and saying, "Who killed my baby, who killed my baby!" It was then that I realized my friend had been killed making deliveries. This was definitely a deterrent for me being a delivery boy. It was a very devastating day. Yes, I cried, because I lost my best friend and teammate.

5

THE NEXT BIG STEP

By the time I made it to high school, my older siblings had dropped out of school, and had begun drinking, doing drugs, selling drugs, and committing other crimes. This lifestyle caused my siblings to go to jail, even prison. As a lonely child, I remember always thinking I had to make it out of this situation and make something of myself. I began to get serious about sports and did enough to get by with my studies. God had always put coaches in my life in little league football and baseball who gave me the confidence to believe I could be somebody. Back in the day, we had a rule in school in order to play sports: "NO PASS, NO PLAY". This became a motivation for me to study and get passing grades. Mind you, I was neither motivated nor educated in understanding what it took to get into college. As a freshman in high school, I decided to try out for basketball, even though I had never played organized basketball before. My brothers and I had played hoops all day every day, many times missing curfew and getting into trouble. I loved basketball, but committed a lot of my time to playing football and baseball. When it came to sports, I didn't experience a lot of failures. I was always a starter and one of the more productive players on a team. Well, my freshman year, I got cut from the basketball team, and the thing I love so much gave me my greatest pain.

We sometimes wonder why our friends and family hurt us so much. It's because our greatest pains come from the things we love the most. How will you handle it? Will it motivate or discourage you? Getting cut in basketball motivated me in a way I had never felt before! I quit football and began to focus on basketball and baseball. I spent every waking day and night playing basketball—literally every night. Many nights, while my mom was out having a good time, I was at the park across the street from my house, playing basketball against the midnight drunks who always wanted to relive their dream. This became a nightly appointment for me— to meet the drunks at the park and play against them for money. Yep, as a young man, I started gambling on playing and winning in basketball. This was a twofold blessing for me. For one, I was able to work on my game against older, more experienced people. I became more and more fearless against my opponent. Secondly, unfortunately or fortunately, it was a way for me to make some money to buy some clothes, shoes, and food.

The next year, I made the basketball team, and my career in basketball began. I continued to play baseball, as well, and made the varsity team in that sport before I did in basketball. This motivated me even more. I became very driven to succeed in basketball, knowing I was probably a better baseball player. As a sophomore on junior varsity, we won the city championship, and the varsity team won the state championship. All signs were looking good to play varsity that next year in baseball and basketball. I was so excited. I felt like I was well on my way to fulfilling my goals and dreams of playing college athletics and getting to the pros.

When it became apparent to me that I was pretty good in sports in high school, I was challenged with the ability to stay focused and be able to do homework and get to practices and games. But my oldest brother,

Willie Leary, saw my potential and offered for me to come live with him in order for me to stay focused and work on my game and try to become something in life.

It was my junior year, and the goal was to start on varsity and start getting recruited by colleges. I spent all summer working hard, from sun-up to sundown—sometimes, until two in the morning—waiting on my mother and my siblings to come home from going out. This was a routine I repeated not only in the summer, but also during the school year sometimes.

Well, big news came out that our head basketball coach was leaving and had taken another job after winning the state championship. This was bad news to me, because the head coach had really liked my talent and had high hopes for me. I was afraid the new coach may not see the same thing in me. One day, at a local gym in the summer before my junior year, I met a coach from Faith West Academy, a private Christian school in suburb of Houston in Katy, Texas. This particular coach—Dave Stallman—admired my skills and talent, so he asked me if I would be interested in attending a private school to play for him. My response was simple: I had and was working very hard to start at the best public school in the state at that time.

I decided to go back to my old school for my junior year, and it was the toughest year I had experienced in every way. My teammates pressured me to drink and do drugs, and the new coach was afraid to play his best players all the time, so he created a rotating system. It was a miserable year for me, and I became very discouraged and began to lose hope.

6

A NEW BEGINNING

In the summer of 1986, my life took a drastic turn, and my basketball career looked bright once again. That summer, Willie took me back to the local gym—Memorial High School—and I met Dave Stallman from Houston Christian Prep and Faith West Academy again. This time, when he approached me and asked if I would like to go to a basketball camp with him and some of his players in Florida, I said yes. In my early years, I had never paid for any fees, and the same thing occurred in attending the basketball camp. I had never been to a camp before, so I was over-excited to go. I asked my mom if I could go, and at first, she said no, because "that white man may take you somewhere and harm you and never bring you back." Willie had also met Coach Stallman and told my mom he was a nice man and just wanted me to come play basketball for him. So, after my continuing to ask her, she finally said yes. I had grown up in places that struggled with racism and discrimination. This is important to note, because this coach was white, and so were all of the players who were attending the camp. The other issue I had was that I didn't own a good pair of tennis shoes, and therefore, Coach gave me a pair of shoes to wear. On the trip to Florida, I noticed all the players were so excited to see the camp director, because he was a hall of fame basketball player! I asked the players and coach, "Whose camp are we attending?" Their response was "Pistol" Pete Maravich and his dad, Press Maravich! I was astounded, and even more excited I was going to meet a professional basketball player and a Hall of Fame player.

We arrived at the camp, and at check in, I must have had the biggest smile in my life! I met Pistol Pete and told him I was going to be the best player at his camp. His response was, "I would like to see that." The first opportunity I had to show Pistol Pete what I had, I made a fool of myself. It was not because of my play—I played great—but my attitude stunk. I was hard on my teammates, and I complained about referee calls. I saw Pistol after we played and asked him what he thought. He replied, "You might be the best player here, but you will never win my most valuable camper with that bad attitude you have." I was shocked, but as in anything, I became more determined to be the best camper. As each day went by, it was clear that I was the best player in camp, but I struggled with my character and attitude. I was very selfish, and quite frankly, mean to my teammates. When they didn't catch my passes, I would yell at them—even though a lot of the passes were my fault, because I was trying to be fancy. I could not overcome my bad attitude toward my teammates and the referees.

Oftentimes, when have a gift to use to impact people in a positive way, we ruin it, and look for an excuse as to why it's someone else's fault. One of the first principles to being successful is "GET OUT OF YOUR OWN WAY!"

Finally, the camp came to a close, and my team was undefeated and positioned to win the camp championship. I just knew, if we won the championship, I would win the MVP. We won the championship, and the awards ceremony was scheduled after dinner, along with a speech from Pistol Pete to bring the camp to a close. On my way to dinner, Pistol

Pete came up to me and asked if I would sit with him for dinner. I said sure, with a big smile! I knew I had made an impression on the Hall of Fame player, and his dad. So, at dinner, Press Maravich told me I was a very good player, and he believed I had a great chance to be a great player. I was so happy. After a bad year at school, I had finally gotten to show someone how good I was and how hard I had worked. The only thing was… I had worked hard on my skills and not my character. So, Pistol Pete said, "You know, Stephon, Dad is right. You are a very good player, and you have a great chance to be a college player, maybe even a professional if you worked hard enough, and stayed out of trouble." Furthermore, he said I reminded him of Tiny Archibald— another NBA great. I was thrilled, and then the air left the room, for Pistol then said, "Tonight, at the awards banquet, you will not receive the MVP."

I said, "Why? Why?" He said his camp was not just about building and teaching skills and drills, but also character, and my character did not reflect the MVP award. I was crushed. After all that hard work, I had come up short again. I got up and left the dinner table angry— so angry, I went and packed my bags and told Coach Stallman I was not going to the awards banquet! I also told him I was leaving the camp and walking home! Like I could really walk from Florida back to Houston. As I was walking toward the exit gate, Coach Stallman caught up to me, sat me down, and explained to me how important it was to have character as a person. In fact, this camp was an opportunity for me to understand that I needed a savior who would change my life and give me the tools to be the best God had created me to be. I asked him to explain more to me, and he did! So, my attitude changed, and I attended the awards ceremony. In closing, Pistol Pete Maravich shared his testimony before the awards were given out. He talked about being a great player and how he had almost lost it all because of bad choices and his character. He said he faced death on a couple occasions by being at the wrong place at the wrong time and running his big mouth. He also talked about how hard he had been on his teammates. Everything he said resonated inside of me. He then closed out his message by telling us how it wasn't until he gave his life to Jesus Christ that he began to understand what life was all about. I was moved by his speech, and as he ended his talk, he offered us the same opportunity to make Jesus Christ our Lord and Savior. I responded to the call, and my life changed from that time on!

Soon after the camp in Florida, Pistol was scheduled to do a camp in Houston, and he personally invited me, and told me I didn't have to pay—someone was going to sponsor my attending the camp. This was a chance for me to redeem myself. I attended the camp in Houston, and this time, my team won the championship and my character changed. I got the MVP award! It was the best day of my life! Pistol Pete and Press were so happy for me, they gave me their phone numbers, and we kept in touch throughout the summer, even until that next summer, when they called me and asked me to be on staff with them for a camp in Houston.

The greatest lesson in my life came through achieving, not failing. If we look close enough, God is interested in using whatever He can to get us to fulfill His purpose and to come to know Him as our Lord and Savior You see, we were created for Him, and Him alone. We were created with divine purpose.

7

NEW LIFE DIVINE INTERVENTION

While at the camp in Houston, I was a friendlier person: I played around with the kids, demonstrated drills, shooting, and dunking for them. There were a couple of kids I played with every day. As I began to prepare to return home, Dave Stallman asked me if I would like to come play for him at the Christian school. I told him I had to talk to my mom. When I got home, I felt so out of place; my spirit on the inside was uncomfortable with my living environment. My mom was not available, my siblings were hustling in the streets, and there were the temptations of alcohol and drugs around the house. I became so uncomfortable, I felt out of place. I asked my mom if I could go stay with Willie, and she said yes. So, I moved in with my brother, thinking I was in a better place to stay out of trouble and not be tempted to make a bad choice. As time went by, it was great, because my oldest brother and I would go any and everywhere to play basketball. However, each night I laid down, there just seemed to be something missing in my life. Since becoming a Christian, I had spent a lot of my spare time reading the Bible Coach Stallman had given me. The emptiness grew stronger the closer it came time to go back to school. I really did not want to go back to my high school. I wanted more for myself, and I also wanted the opportunity to get a scholarship to pursue my dream of playing college basketball and, perhaps, professional basketball. I began to believe the gift I had as a basketball player could be used to help provide a better life for my family. On one particular day, I called Coach Stallman and told him I would like to visit the school, if he could come and pick me up. I asked my mom and my brother if it was okay for me to go check out this Christian school in Katy. My mom's first response was, "How are you going to get to Katy every day to go to school?"

I responded, "I don't know, Mom, but I feel like I'm supposed to go check it out." Little did I know, on my visit, the most miraculous thing happened in my life. I went to a five a.m. prayer meeting with Coach Stallman, and while at this meeting, I met a very nice couple who asked me what was I doing at the prayer service. I responded that I was visiting the school with Coach Stallman to determine if I was going to transfer or not. So, I visited the school, and I liked the opportunity it could give me. So, I asked Coach where I would live? He then told me the family I had met at the prayer, Dave and Lynne Johnson, told him while we were praying that God had spoken to them and said if I was going to attend the school, they would like to offer me a place to live. I was amazed, yet perplexed, because they didn't know me—and once again, they were white, and I was a black kid from the inner city. Amazed by the news, I felt completely at peace to leave my high school and spend my senior year in Katy, attending Houston Christian and living with this family. Before I decided to return home, Coach Stallman told me the family offered me to come have dinner with them and meet their other kids. So, before I went home, I went over to their house to meet them.

God is always a mile ahead of us. While I was debating on what I should do about my senior year and the school I would attend, God had a preordained plan. You see, God has a plan for you, the goals and dreams we have—He placed them there. It is our responsibility to be obedient enough to walk down the path He has prepared for you. Are you wondering what you should do next? I encourage you to read the Word, pray, and start your journey, God is already ahead of you, working out the details. In essence, your goals and dreams are waiting on you! Psalms 37:4 says, "Delight yourself in the Lord, and He will give you the desires of your heart."

8

LOVE AND FAMILY

This family, the Johnsons, invited me to their house for dinner to meet the rest of the family. When I arrived, I was again amazed because the kids I had played with at camp were the sons and daughter of Lynne and Dave Johnson. I began to really think there must be a God, only He could bring about this coincidence. I had a wonderful time at dinner, and the kids took to me very well. They began to affirm what I was really there for by saying, "Mom and Dad, can Stephon come live with us and be our big brother?" For the first time, I felt a love and acceptance like no other. Immediately, I had forgotten I was black, and they were white. The power of God changes the eyes, the heart, and the spirit of a man.

In an instant, my faith had grown immensely. I began to believe God had a plan for me, and He was sure to lead me down the path I needed to travel. If He could give me this hope and belief, He can do the same for you. Just believe!

Well, there was just one more hurdle: permission from my mom. So, I returned home, and she was there, waiting to hear about my trip. I told her about my decision to follow Christ, and this coach and family wanted me to come live with them and go to this private Christian school. In spite of my mom not being around because she worked two jobs and went out to have a good time on occasion, I knew she was proud of my accomplishments, and even though she couldn't be at my games, she wanted me to be successful.

My mom's first response was no, "I don't know those people, I don't know where you're going, and I don't know what those white people may do to you." After I told her I wasn't comfortable being at home, going to the school I was attending, and playing for the new coach plus the crime, drugs, alcohol, the playing opportunity, and that Houston Christian would give me a better education to go to college and earn a scholarship. My mom changed her mind, and there I was, on my way to a stranger's house and to a new school.

When God opens a door, don't ask questions, just be obedient and faithful to the call. Everyone's calling will not be the same, because there is divine purpose in the calling. It happened to me almost instantaneously: God began to give me a new vision for my life—one that was filled with breaking color barriers, importance of education, and a life of character. Don't expect your calling to be like your parents' or your friends' callings. Look for God to do something just for you!

When I got to the Johnsons' home, they all greeted me with a hug, kiss, and smiles. It was the greatest feeling I have ever felt. It was the first time someone hugged me, and even kissed me on the cheek! They soon showed me my room and bed. For the first time in my life, I had my own bed and my own room. My life got so much better as the Johnsons showed me true love and what family was all about. Plus, they helped me grow as a Christian, helped me understand the importance of education, and helped me learn how to make good decisions in life. I also learned lessons such as doing chores and being rewarded for working around the house. My greatest memory came when I went to bed for the first time: we had family prayer, and everyone prayed for one another, and the troubles of this world. After prayer, everyone would hug each other and say goodnight. My fondest memory is my sister, Jessica, came and jumped in the bed, gave me a big hug and a kiss, and told me she loved me and was glad I was here. Wow, it still warms my heart today, and she will always be my lil' sis who loved and kissed me from day one! Today, I still have my days where I make a stop at TJ Maxx, because after finishing our chores on Saturdays, Mom used to ask, "Who wants to go shopping! I'll buy you something!" I would always go along to shop, so today, I tell everyone my shopping habits are from Lynne. On my first shopping trip, Mom brought a color chart to see which colors would look the best against my skin, and today, I shop for those same colors. My life had completely changed. Soon, it was time for me to attend school and pick my grades up, so I could get a scholarship to play in college and pursue my dream of being a pro. The Johnsons were kind enough to take me home to meet and see my family and assure my mother I was okay. They even helped me get my license and allowed me to drive their car home on the weekends to visit.

I finally felt like there was meaning to life. As a child refusing to participate in crimes, drugs, and alcohol, I always felt like I was a stranger in a foreign country, but now, I had a reason to believe and know why I should make such choices. Life was amazing; God is truly good. My senior year, I applied myself to my studies and gave myself a schedule for when my homework had to be done before I could go out and play basketball. That was a tough adjustment, because as you can remember, there were times I stayed out all night playing with the drunks. I now had a curfew and certain time I had to go to bed. All of which gave me the discipline I had been missing all my life.

I had the best year of my life. I was a heavily recruited basketball player. I was recruited by such schools as Texas A&M, Baylor, and University Arkansas—I even received calls from North Carolina and Indiana. I made a 4.0 in my classes, and I made the necessary score on the SAT to qualify for college. I also grew tremendously as a young Christian! Our team was like the story of Hoosiers. We had 12 kids in our senior class—it was a very small school—but we had a very good team. We won many tournaments, district championships, and made it to the state championship game before falling short. Because of our successful season, we were invited to the NACA Christian School National Tournament in Tennessee. We brought home a six-foot trophy after winning the championship. I was named MVP and All American. I could not have dreamed of a better senior year. I was also first team all-state player. After a very successful season of going to the state championship game and winning the national championship, I was undecided on what college I should attend. I took visits to schools, but found no peace. I was a looking for something different than just playing basketball. So, one day I called Pistol Pete and Press Maravich for advice.

Pete told me some depressing news: he told me his father had passed away. I was crushed. Press had taken an interest in me and had seen my potential to be great. He then told me if there was a place where he could play Division One basketball and grow as a Christian, that's what he would do. At the time, I didn't feel like I had that option, so I put off signing until I was sure what I should do. The one thing I had confidence in was God had not brought me that far to turn back.

Sometimes, along the journey to reaching your destiny and fulfilling your dreams and goals, you may face some days of uncertainty. Don't give up hope; don't lose heart!

Philippians 1:6 says, "Being confident of this very thing, He that began a good work in you will be faithful to complete it." You see, God has your steps ordered, just keep walking forward.

I received an invitation to attend a camp where players were being invited to go to Australia to play teams that would increase exposure and witness to the people, all while representing the USA. The camp was in Tennessee. While at this camp, one of Liberty University's coaching staff approached me about being an unsigned player and asked me why. I told him I was just waiting on the right opportunity for me. It was important I had confidence in the university to develop me as a man, not just a basketball player. The coach explained to me that Liberty was a Christian university in Virginia, and they were still looking for a point guard. When I returned home, I got the package in the mail, and everything the university stood for seemed to be the place for me. After my dad, Dave Johnson, looked over the information and spoke to the coaches, it became apparent that I was headed to Liberty University! I was offered a full scholarship to play basketball, and I had the chance to lead this new Division One Christian University to new heights! Once again, God had a plan, and it took going to Tennessee to walk right into my next step on my journey.

I often tell people now, "Do not doubt in the valley that God promises on the mountain top!" Put your faith and trust in Him! He will never leave you, never forsake you!

What an amazing year in my life. I had one bigger thing to accomplish: graduating from high school. I decided in the spring, since the school was so small and they needed more baseball players, that I would join the team. This would be icing on the cake to finish out my senior year, playing the sport I had played most of my life before falling in love with basketball. This became one of the most remarkable things I could have done, because God gave me a glimpse of where I had come from, where I was, and where He was taking me. I was a picture for my team, and on this particular day, we were playing Westbury Christian. A batter was walking up to the plate, and he looked at me, and I looked at him. All of a sudden, I heard a voice from the stands, and it was my little league coach, because that was his son who at bat. What a reunion! You see, this coach was the coach who had picked me up for practice and had made it possible for me to play little league. More importantly, he and his family fed me and let me spend a night to make sure I could make the games. This coach was also the one who would tell me, "Stay out of trouble. You have a gift, and you could be special. Stay away from the drugs, alcohol, and crime." In the middle of the game, it stopped for a moment and gave me a chance to say hello and collect my thoughts. So, you see, God comes through again. He affirmed the decision I made to not only attend Houston Christian, but also to play baseball. After the game, we hugged and cried. Coach was so happy to see me make it out of the inner city.

The most exciting thing was yet to come. Graduating from high school would be a first in my family, and so was attending a university on a scholarship. I had one small challenge: since Houston Christian was a Christian school, I needed a Bible class to graduate, so upon the announcement of those who were able to graduate, I was told I needed to complete this course before I could. This was a minor setback, and I had one month to complete a year's worth of school. I worked day and night to complete homework, tests, and quizzes to finish the course. I did it, and I got an A! Now, I could call my mom and tell her I was graduating. This was big for my mom, because she had never had time to attend anything I had done before, so I wasn't sure she would attend. Well, the big day came, and my mom, my sister—Stephanie, my mom's boyfriend, and my oldest brother came to support me. A journey complete, this was a monumental experience. My mom was very proud that I had made the decision to leave home to pursue my goals and dreams. This phenomenal year was capped off by me receiving the Athlete of the Year award, because of the one thing I had not had when I had first attended Pistol Pete's camp: **character!**

There will be clear evidence of change when you submit your life to Christ. He will make you new, and give you a new perspective on life. A life from the inside out, not the outside in! "It is Christ in you that is the Hope of Glory,"— Colossians 1:27!

Overcoming the Challenge of Race Relations "A Bridge over wavy waters."

It was a big step for Dave and Lynne Johnson to invite a young black man into their home. You would think that in 1986, there was not much racism. However, this was one of the adjustments I needed to make, not only living in Katy, but also in going back home, where I was also judged. At that time, there was a popular show, called *Different Strokes*, which had two, African-American young men living with a single parent dad and his daughter. There were several times that someone would walk up to me and call me Willis or Arnold, and even make the statement of the popular slogan Arnold said: "What you talking about Willis?" In one part of the world, I was being teased as an African-American young man living with a white family and being accused of acting "white" or talking "white", while in the other part of my life, I was being discriminated against. There was one particular time that my childhood friend, Albert Freeman, came out to the Johnson's house to spend the night with me, and as we turned into the neighborhood, there was a cop who followed the car all the way until we got home. When we stepped out of the car and started to walk toward the back door—which is the door Mom Lynne left open whenever I came back at a later time—the officer got out of the car and questioned Albert and I, as if I did not live there. I told him I was living at the house, and Albert was spending the night with me. The officer did not believe us and made us lay on the ground. While this was happening, the lights of his car woke Mom Lynne up, and she came outside, saw the officer, and asked what we had done wrong. The officer responded, "I found these two young men getting ready to go into your back door."

Mom Lynne said, "Well, that's our son and his friend. You have made a tremendous mistake." This was a terrifying experience for Albert and I, but one we both still discuss today. It taught us a valuable lesson in our lives about race relations. There were other times when I began to drive the cars of the family, and if I got pulled over, the officers would not believe I had the right to drive those cars and would accuse me of stealing the cars. I was harassed until I was able to prove I had the right. It even got to the point where I asked Dave Pops to write a letter, so I could keep it in the car in case I got stopped. When I watch the news and hear about racism in America, I'm always taken back to a time and place where I learned some valuable lessons about loving and accepting others. I know what it felt like to be the only African-American young man or person in a room or restaurant and having people stare at you as if you don't belong. In one case, we stopped at a restaurant as we travelled to Dallas, and I went up to play a video game with my siblings. The kid who was playing was white, and his parents called him to come back to the table when I walked up. I didn't know how to receive or take these situations, but Dave and Lynne always made sure I felt like I was part of the family, that they loved me, and my siblings did the same thing, as well. I was taught that racism and discrimination was something of the past that was taught to people, and while many have still acted in ignorance, we must choose to love.

There was never a time when they treated me or made me feel like I was of another race or ethnicity. They treated me like I was one of them. I believe that shaped and formed me into the man I am today: I don't see race; I see everyone as God's loving creation. It is also a challenge in which I employ the rest of America to love one another to look beyond the color of our skin, and not judge one another because of their in ethnicity, but let love be the guiding source of all of our relationships.

9

THE COLLEGE YEARS: MY FIRST REAL CHALLENGE

My life was great. Here I was, a young man from a small town in Louisiana, who had grown up in the inner city of Houston, Texas, now attending a Division One Christian university, playing basketball, and pursuing a college education. Who would have ever thought a kid with the last name "Leary or Coleman" would end up at a university playing college basketball? Growing up there were many people who doubted I would be where I am today. Upon arriving at Liberty University, I had the pleasure and the honor of my dad (Dave) taking me to school—mind you, Liberty University was in Lynchburg, Virginia. This required Dad to take off work and leave the rest of the family. I can't tell you how much this meant to me, as a young man who had grown up without a father. You see, after graduation, the Johnson family had sat me down and had a long conversation concerning my future. The year they had offered me to come and live with them to attend school was over. Now, it was time for me to return home, but they offered me the opportunity to permanently become part of the family. I was blown away and overwhelmed with joy. My sisters and brothers were all in: it was a unanimous choice to have me be part of the family for life. We discussed the specifics of adopting me into the family, because they wanted to support me getting through college and finding my purpose, and to help me be successful. You can only imagine the joy, tears, and love we all shared that day. It is the same love we still feel today. What an awesome God we serve! How much does God love us that He would put someone in my path to love me and help me discover my purpose in this life?

So, Dad and I arrived on campus, and we faced our first odd perception of who I was and who the white man was with me. The funniest thing happened our first night in the dorm. My then-roommate, Tim Scarborough, arrived on campus, and Dad and I stayed in the dorm room that night. When Tim came into the room, I just so happened to be in the restroom, so Tim saw this older, white gentleman in the room. He began to wonder, "Who is the old guy in my room? I thought the new recruit was a point guard who was a black kid!" Startled by my dad's presence, Tim thought he was in the wrong room, and began to turn around and walk out, when my dad said, "Are you looking for Stephon?" Tim responded yes, so Dad said, "He is in the restroom. Hi, I'm his dad, Dave Johnson." When I returned to the room, we laughed so hard over that situation. It was then that I realized that me being adopted by a white family was going to be a great opportunity to share how good God is.

Along the journey to discovering your purpose, God will show you meaningful things that only you will be able to comprehend. Do not expect others to know and understand your purpose. Keep your eyes open and your spirit ready! Pray this simple prayer, "Open the eyes of my heart, Lord, that I may see your goodness in the land of the living!"

I felt I was one big step from my dream of playing professional basketball. In the first couple of months I was at Liberty, I was called into the office by Coach Meyer. He told me some heartbreaking news; he said, "The

Dean of Students would like to see you, because it was just announced that the Hall of Fame basketball player, Pistol Pete Maravich, has died while playing basketball with Dr. James Dobson." I cried like a baby—after all, this man had played a big role in my life changing. He had sent me letters of encouragement, and he had believed in me. Most of all, it was his message that had led me to Christ. I reported to the dean, where I had the opportunity to speak with Dr. Dobson about what Pistol Pete meant to me. I had lost a great friend and mentor.

Playing college basketball was no easy thing. I struggled to learn the new system and workouts. My body did not know how to handle that punishment, because I had never worked out like that before. Right before the season started, the starting line-up was announced, and I was not in it. I was very hurt and disappointed. I called my guardian family and talked to Mom and Dad. They comforted me and told me to hang in there—to keep honoring God, and He would honor me. So, I accepted the challenge of coming off the bench. By the fifth game of the season, coach Jeff Meyer announced the starting line-up and said, "We are making a change. Stephon, you will start as point guard."

Just when I thought things were going well, I received some more bad news. Just before I was to get on the bus to leave for a game, my oldest brother called to tell me my biological father had passed away, and I needed to come home. I was hurt by the news and cried, but my father and I had not had a relationship. He had lived in Louisiana and had never come to visit us as kids, and when we would go to see him, he never took a lot of time with me. Nevertheless, it was another disappointment in my life. I told my brother we were on our way to a game, and I would call to find out the funeral details when we got back. Coach asked me if I would like to stay at school and handle my situation, and I said no, I needed to go with my team. I played with a heavy heart that game, but I played well. When I returned to school, I called to find out the details of the funeral, but before I called, I prayed for peace and strength. My mom and my brother—Gladys and Willie—told me the plans and told me I needed to come home as soon as possible. For some unknown reason, I told my mom and brother I did not plan on missing school and games to come to the funeral. I told them it was important for me to stay, and I would visit the gravesite when I got a break at school. They were shocked and amazed, but surprisingly, they understood my position.

You see I had written my father a letter just a couple of months before he passed away, explaining that I loved him and had forgiven him for not being the dad I had needed him to be. I explained to him that I had become a Christian, and I needed to follow the scriptures and forgive those who had hurt me, in order for Christ to forgive me. I told him I loved him, and maybe one day, we could have a relationship. My dad never responded to that letter, but I felt a great peace when I wrote it and mailed it off. I later discovered from my grandmother when I visited the gravesite that my dad had carried that letter around with him, and it was one of the last things sitting by his bedside when he died. I knew then that God had prepared me for that situation before I had known it would happen.

After being named a starter, I was so ecstatic again that my perseverance and hard work had paid off. I remained starter for the remainder of the year. I had a great freshman year—some good games, some bad games. However, I was able to finish the year with a promising future.

Upon returning home, I was faced with the decision of going back to the inner city or back out to the Johnson's. On one hand, this appeared to be an easy decision. However, I was torn between two worlds. Liberty was a very strict university when it came to rules of curfew, what we could watch on TV, or listen to on the radio. My two worlds were forcing me to think I needed some freedom, and that freedom was with my biological family—but that came with a steep price: tolerating the lifestyle of sex, gambling, drugs, alcohol, and crime. Meanwhile, I knew returning to the Johnsons' was the best thing for me, but I knew that if I did, I had to get a job and abide by the rules.

I decided to go to the Johnsons', but I delayed getting a job, because I was always playing basketball and running around with friends. Sooner rather than later, Mom and Dad sat me down and told me I needed to get a job to put away funds for school and pay for insurance if I was going to keep driving the cars. So, I did get a job and loved the idea of making money so much, I got a second job. But the one thing that suffered was training and working on my game. I came to a crossroads and told Mom and Dad I really needed to be working out and training to get ready for school, but they thought I needed to work, as well. It was a very complex situation for me, because I felt like my goal was to play professional basketball, but how could I be the best player I was capable of being if I wasn't training or working out enough?

Things got to the point where I became very frustrated, and I told Mom and Dad I was going back to the inner city. So, I did, and that turned out to be a bad situation. While I was home, the cops knocked on the door and pushed the door in, looking for someone who may have robbed the flea market. It had been reported that the person lived in mom's apartment. That was a very scary moment for me—so much, it scared me straight. I told my mom I had made a mistake, and if I was going to make something of myself, it was best for me to live with the Johnsons. She totally understood and gave me her blessing. So, I had to humble myself and ask the Johnsons, "May I please come back home?" And of course, they said yes, with open arms. So, I returned to the Johnsons', got a job, and finished the summer trying my best to work and workout.

Sometimes, God teaches us harsh lessons. He allows us to make decisions He knows are not the right ones. However, it leads us back to His purpose and plan for our lives. Also, Mom and Dad taught me the greatest lesson as an inner-city kid, and that was learning the value of hard work and making a living.

My sophomore year came around, and I was very excited to return to school. I was expected to start again, but I had not spent my summer working hard and developing my game, so I had some catching up to do when I got back to school. I reported to school out of shape. Well, to say the least, my sophomore year was very difficult. Although I felt like I caught up to my old self, I was benched for another player for what I thought was favoritism, and my relationship with Coach Meyer was contentious. I felt like my dream was fading away. Phone calls to Mom and Dad were not working! I felt like giving up. I cried out to God and felt like He didn't hear me, either. After all, every effort I made to better my situation and win my starting job back, brought more tension between Coach Meyer and me. I was coming off the bench producing and out-playing the starting guard, but Coach Meyer was trying to teach me a lesson. A lesson I was having a problem understanding, so I began to get bitter and not care about basketball, or life. My dream was being shattered.

I remember at one home game, we were losing bad, and Coach Meyer was making a point that he was not going to play me because of my attitude! I was a well-liked person and player at Liberty, so the crowd starting chanting, "We want Steph! We want Steph!" The chant was loud, and it was a satisfying feeling to know that people saw my talent and efforts and appreciated me. On the other hand, Coach Meyer did not like it and came down to the bench and accused me of making the students cheer for me.

He said, "How dare you do something like this! For that, you will sit the rest of the game." I was crushed in my spirit. I had never felt so low in my athletic career! I grew more and more bitter and did not care anymore. I thought, "It's over. I will never play again."

The very next home game, the same thing occurred, and the students chanted for me again. This time, he waited until the last two minutes of the game, and we were down 12 points. I thought, "Okay! Here is my big chance." I checked into the game with a standing ovation from the crowd. It was a great feeling to be loved and appreciated. My first opportunity, I stole the ball and made a three-point shot. We pressed and got another steal and scored, and just like that, we were down by seven, with a minute-and-a-half to go. My teammates and I scrambled and pressed hard: we stole the ball, and I scored another three-pointer. We had cut the lead to four. We fought hard and came back and won the game. It was a great feeling; the crowd rushed the floor as we celebrated a tremendous comeback. All I could think was that I was sure to get my starting position back now. At the practice the next day, Coach Meyer mentioned the spirited effort that we gave to win that game, but said that we would stick with the same guys who had been starting. You can imagine that by now, I was fed up.

Liberty was a strict university at the time, and the rules of the university were often hard to uphold. I began to push the issue with some of the rules, rebelling against my RAs. I was in a very serious relationship at the time, and I began to drift away from the game of basketball. I became more and more bitter that my dream was fading away. Spring break came around, and I decided to spend spring break with my girlfriend and her family. Due to an institutional policy, when we returned from spring break a day later than expected—even though we had had parental permission—we had to go see the Dean of Students for discipline. It was decided that I needed a semester out of school to think about whether Liberty was place for me! I was devastated—all my hopes and dreams gone down the tube. I lost everything I had worked so hard for! I had overcome so many things to get to where I was. The only thing I thought was, why was God allowing this to happen to me? What was once supposed to be a great sophomore year, continuing my dream of playing college ball and eventually getting to the NBA, had turned into my walls coming tumbling down.

10

RETURNING HOME AFTER BEING SUSPENDED A SEMESTER

I was so ashamed of having to return from school. I had lost my scholarship, my chance to get a college degree, and my dream of playing college basketball, let alone professional basketball. I thought my life was over. The most difficult thing was for me to face my mom and siblings, who had looked up to me and had wanted so bad to see someone in the family be successful. Of course, because they did not understand what Liberty was all about, they could not understand why I had been dismissed from school. They thought I had been mistreated. Now what should I do, what could I do? Life was filled with so many unanswered questions! The only thing I knew to do was trust God, and I wasn't even sure what that meant! The best thing for me was to continue to live with the Johnson family and allow their love and encouragement to help me grow as a Christian. I got involved in Church activities, helping with the youth and even sharing my testimony. I began to gain some strength and started to believe again that God loved me and had a purpose for my life. I started calling all the universities to explain my situation, and of course, because those other schools were not strict, they understood my dilemma. I also joined some leagues and performed well against many professional players. I was approached by a couple of agents about playing overseas and making hundreds of thousands of dollars. I was excited about that possibility, and they also told me if I performed well overseas, there was still a chance to play in the NBA.

I told my mom (Gladys) about it, and she approved of me to do whatever I thought was best for me. So, I told the Johnson family about my opportunity, and their first question was, "What about your education?" They further asked me what had been the response of the other schools? I responded that there was interest by three schools, including returning to Liberty! You see, Coach Meyer had called me and asked what my plan was and explained how he felt he had handled my situation wrong, that he would love for me to return to Liberty under one circumstance—that I take a cut in my scholarship the first semester. But if I followed all the rules and stayed out of trouble, I would get my full scholarship the second semester.

Mom and Dad were excited, but I was not particularly excited about returning to Liberty. I wanted to play overseas and make a lot money to begin helping my family get out of the inner city. Mom and Dad explained how if I had unforgiveness or bitterness in my heart toward Liberty or Coach Meyer, I would never be free to be successful.

I prayed over the options that were before me, and the Johnsons prayed with me. I felt this overwhelming peace that I was supposed to go back to Liberty, even though there was a price to pay. On one hand, I didn't think I deserved to suffer because of the strict rules or Coach Meyer's decisions, but on the other hand, I had to take responsibility for my own actions. Something I remember Pistol Pete taught me about my attitude at camp and why I did not get the MVP award. Mom and Dad told me that they would financially help me get through college—if I returned to Liberty under those circumstances! Oh, there was one other stipulation: I had to sit out the coming year, because the school took my second semester grades away from me, therefore making me ineligible to compete the following year. It was an NCAA rule, and there was no way around it. Also, I needed to go to summer school to pull my GPA up to give me a chance to be eligible for the following year. This was a tough situation for me to accept, but I really felt God wanted me to return to Liberty!

11

BACK AT LIBERTY

Well, as you can imagine, having to return to a place where you had been dismissed wasn't easy. I had to look everyone in the eye and apologize and take responsibility for my actions. Never mind what the opinions were about the school's ruling or even how Coach Meyer had treated me. For the most part, I was well received by everyone, but especially by the student body who cheered me on the court. I faced many challenges I did not have to face as a full scholarship athlete.

First, check-in was a hassle; I didn't have the same advisor making sure I had the classes I needed to be eligible. I didn't get the one teammate-roommate, I felt like I made the wrong decision, but I could not turn back. This was the second chance I had prayed for. The school year began, and off-season practice started. I wanted to make sure I finished every drill first; I wanted to be the best in everything. I ran the fastest times. I had gotten so much stronger in the weight room, so I was lifting with the big men. My next challenge was on the court: could I keep a good attitude when things didn't go my way, and could I become the leader I was meant to be? Official practice had begun, and the first thing I had to swallow was that it was not important for me to do certain drills. I had to sit on the sidelines and watch my teammates. I was bored—

and sometimes, discouraged—but I had to rise above it all. So, I started cheering for my teammates to work hard and get better. All of a sudden, it clicked: I was in this position to learn how to encourage others. It was not about me; it was about the team and my teammates.

Throughout the year, it was difficult, but I managed to keep trying to allow God to change me. I was responsible for being on the scout team, the team that imitated the up-and-coming opponents. I was always the scorer on the opposing team. I took advantage of showing coach just what he was missing. I shot lights out every opportunity I got and scored at will. My teammates were upset, because they felt I was trying to get them in trouble, but my job was to prepare them and make them better, as well earn my scholarship back.

The end of the semester came: I had a 3.2 GPA, and I had never had one incident. Coach Meyer called me into the office, and he was a man of his word; he gave me my scholarship back and told me he was very pleased with my work ethic, attitude, and skills. Even though I was not playing in the games, I felt like I was finally back. I called Mom and Dad, and told them the good news. They were very proud of me, and we thanked God I was growing and learning valuable lessons. Because they were so proud, they sent me an allowance each month to continue to make school enjoyable. I was ecstatic and excited about the possibility of achieving my goals and dreams. I maintained a good attitude and had good grades the second semester, as well, and then, I was reinstated by the NCAA Eligibility Rules Committee. I had overcome life's greatest challenge before me once again. God is good!

12

FROM THE MOUNTAIN TOP
TO THE VALLEY LOW

I worked harder than I ever had the summer before that school year. I had a second chance to get a college degree, to play college basketball, and to ultimately play professional basketball. I played in four different leagues and worked, while also running and lifting weights regularly. This was sure to be my best year yet. I returned to Liberty with all expectations to start and lead Liberty to a conference championship, which was my goal when I had first decided to attend.

I was doing great, playing better than ever, being a leader, and having a great attitude. There was only one problem: at the end of each day, I had to ice my knee, because it would lock up on me. I thought it was no big deal, so I continued workouts, not wanting to miss a beat earning my job back. Coming out of workouts, I was considered as the starter, but my knee got worse. So, Coach said before the season started, we should get it checked out to make sure I was okay. We scheduled an eight a.m. appointment, so if everything was okay, I would still be able to make it to class and practice. I was asked to sign off on a waiver that if they saw something that needed immediate attention, I would give them the right to perform surgery.

I only remember falling asleep, then waking up as I was rolled out the door while it was dark outside. With Coach Meyer by my side, the only words I could utter were, "Oh no, I had major surgery," and I started to cry. There I was, once again facing another mountain in my life, and having the realization my goals and dreams were fading. After the anesthesia wore off the next day, I met with the trainer, where he explained that my bone that connects my femur and knee was cracked, and I was out for the season and may never play again. He further explained that I had six screws in my knee, holding it together. I was completely devastated and cried like a baby. He further explained that I could not put any weight on my leg for six to nine weeks, depending on my progress. I had to use crutches until the doctor cleared me. My world had come tumbling down. Everything I had worked so hard for, gone— just like that.

I cried, "Why, God, are you doing this to me? I called my Mom and Dad, and my mom, Gladys. They were all sympathetic, but nothing could heal the hurt I felt inside. As it had before when I had faced a difficult time, bitterness began to build up inside of me. I did not know what to do with my dreams being shattered. I began to find joy in dating and going to parties, even though I could not dance. My grades began to suffer again, and I was rebellious against the Liberty rules. I continued on this rebellion journey for a couple of months, until one of the parties I attended was busted by the deans and RAs. While on crutches, I knew it was over for me, thinking, "Here I go again, dismissed from school!" I went and hid behind a tree, hoping and praying they didn't see me. As far as I know, I was seen, but at the very next chapel, it was rumored that over 100 students would be dismissed from school. The deans were going to call out names in chapel, and those who were on the list were immediately expelled from school. I sat in chapel, nervous and afraid. This was a turning point in my life; I realize if I didn't get my act together, not only would I not play professional basketball, but I would not even graduate from college. I was only a year-and-a-half away. I immediately began to thank God for opening my eyes and getting my priorities together.

I went to the doctor for a checkup, and the news was good: my bone was back intact, but I could only walk—no jumping. I began to rehab my way back. I was excited for the news and began to focus on getting back on the court. I worked hard in rehab. The pain was excruciating, as I had lost every ounce of muscle I had built up over time. I went from squatting over 500 pounds, to not being able to do the bar. On leg extensions, I went from doing the whole stack, to not being able to do 10 pounds! Wow! I was starting from ground zero!

Don't doubt in the valley what God promised on the mountain top. The valley represents the path to your higher mountain!

13

THE ROAD TO RECOVERY AND BACK ON THE COURT

It was November when I began my rehab, and my goal was to get back on the court by the beginning of conference play, which was the first week of January. Rehab was tough. It was the most difficult thing I had ever physically done. My trainer and doctor were pleased with my progress. They said I had great muscle memory. My legs were responding to the treatment well, and my goal was intact. The next challenge was learning to run and cut again. Although I had major knee surgery, I never had any ligament damage.

The scary thing in my mind was jumping and coming down on that knee and the possibility of cracking it again. The only thing I knew to do was pray and ask God for strength! I began jogging and doing cutting drills, and everything was going well! By the time January rolled around, I was not ready to test my knee, which was a disappointment. But I had to stay positive and keep working hard! Finally, at the end of January, I got a release to return to the court. I can still remember that feeling today of when I checked into the game and made my first three-pointer! So, I finished the season as a role player off the bench, but I was just happy to be back playing on the court. I had worked and fought so hard to play the game I love so dearly.

By far, the most difficult thing I ever had to do was rehabilitate and get back to the basketball court. I would be remiss if I didn't say I was very angry at God and life for having to endure such a devastating injury when my basketball career and college had gotten off to such a great start. It was a time when I went to a place in the mountain in Lynchburg, Virginia. This place was called the bald spot, because it was the highest place in the mountain had no trees. As students, we used to go up there just to chill out.

On this particular night, I went to the spot and yelled and screamed at God for allowing this injury to happen to me. At the same time, I was also crying and begging for him to give me the strength to overcome it and heal, so I could continue on my journey of playing professional basketball. I worked really hard in rehab and got back to a place where I was 100-percent. Thanks to my trainers who pushed me and instilled in me a desire that drove me to embrace the pain, so I could get back to the court.

14

THE END OF ONE DREAM, THE BEGINNING OF A PURPOSE-FILLED LIFE

Well, off-season started, and I began to experience the same sort of pain and fatigue in my knee! I was advised to stop workouts and let the doctor look at it. I set an appointment, and we went through the same procedure, so I signed off, giving the doctor permission to fix whatever the issue was. Three hours passed, and I woke up, knowing in my heart it was over! It was a tearful moment, and tough to swallow, but I fully understood that life goes on! The one thing that was left was to become the first Leary to graduate from college. I had one year left of eligibility, but only 24 hours to graduate. Since I was on scholarship, Coach Meyer asked me to spend time in the office as a student assistant coach, so I agreed to his requirement.

My senior year, I was at the end of what seemed to be a long journey. My dream of playing in the NBA was over, but I began to think about coaching! My responsibilities included: overseeing workouts, participating in individual workouts and practice, and keeping stats at home games. I loved my schedule— I only had a few classes—and I was still involved in basketball! I finished the first semester on the Dean's list, and I was down to six hours to graduate, it was a great feeling! Needless to say, I finished the year on top: I was on the graduation list. It was an overwhelming feeling. I immediately called my parents and gave them the good news. They were so proud of me, and I asked if they were coming to my graduation. They told me they had some good news and told me they had given my mom (Gladys) money to rent a car to come see me graduate! It was a very unselfish and generous thing for them to do! This was going to be a very significant event in my family heritage. Graduation was everything I thought it would be. It was the happiest I had been in a long time.

God has a unique purpose for each of us, and this relates to our distinctive temperaments, abilities, experiences, spiritual gifts, education, and our spheres of influence.

15

AFTER COLLEGE

My experience in becoming a Christian was unique. However, ever since that time, through spending time reading and studying God's word, it was made very clear to me what my overall purpose was. But I did not know what my specific calling was. One day, I was praying, and I felt a strong sense of God's presence. I began to write four things down on paper: "First, I am establishing a Christian heritage to be carried out from generation to generation. Second, I am establishing an educational heritage. Third, I am building a life of successful heritage. And fourth, I am building a marriage and family heritage through you, my son."

I have held these four things near and dear to my heart until this day. At that time, it didn't mean much to me, but as I matured as a Christian young man, and learned what a heritage and a generation was in the scriptures, it became clear to me that God had plucked me out of my family to establish and build a heritage and generation. That was exciting to know. However, it has been challenging. You see, even when we know our purpose, and we get excited about what God has in store for us, we must realize that there is an enemy who wants to keep us from walking in God's will for our lives.

Jesus said it best in John 10:10, "The thief cometh to kill, steal, and destroy, but I come that you might have life and have it more abundantly."

Returning home a college graduate was a thrilling feeling, but I would be remiss if I didn't admit I missed playing the game I love. While I was overseeing the weight training program, I was also rehabbing and training myself. My knee was feeling really good—the best it had felt in a long time. So, I joined a pro-am team to see if I could play at a high level again. Surprisingly, I still could play with the big boys. I scored 48 points my first game, and 60 the second. There was an NBA agent in the crowd who approached me after the game and wanted to know my situation. I told them about my career at Liberty and wouldn't mind playing professional ball. This NBA agent was named Tony Dutt, and he and I became great friends. I even worked with him years later. Tony and I exchanged numbers that day, and he took me to a workout session at HBU, where the Rockets worked out. He later set me up go to San Antonio for a workout with the Spurs. Although I could play well on several days and shoot really well, the grinding on my knee was too much to overcome. It became apparent my knee would not hold up. I can have a good day playing against the best, but doing so day after day took its toll on my knee. I could finally put that dream to bed and enjoy the playing game in summer and men's leagues.

While playing in a men's league, we played against a Harlem Globetrotter by the name of Willie "Sky" Foreman, and his friend, Reggie Harrison, who was a referee for the Globetrotters. I had one of those great shooting nights of making 15 threes, and after the game, I was approached by the two gentlemen. They asked who I was and where I was playing. I responded, "Nowhere. I had a couple knee surgeries, and I just play for fun. These two guys thought I was still good enough to play overseas or even play with the Globetrotters as a shooter and ballhandler with fancy passes. It was humbling to be thought of in that way. This men's league allowed me to regain some confidence, as I was scoring 40 points on a nightly basis. Reggie was a witness to these games, because he was refereeing. He told me, "Stephon, man, you need to be overseas. I'm gonna make some calls for you."

My hope and dream of playing professional ball was reborn. Willie invited me to a Globetrotter workout, where I met the great "Sweet Lou" Dunbar. It was an honor to be among these guys. However, the Globetrotter experience wasn't going to work out, as the roster was already full.

Meanwhile, Reggie did his best to connect me overseas, but to no avail. Tony Dutt reappeared in the picture when he was utilizing the West Houston Athletic Club as a place to work guys out, and this is the place where I was playing in the men's pro-am. Tony also saw a few more of my performances and tried to find me a place to play overseas, but it just wasn't meant be. Willie, Reggie, Tony, and even Sweet Lou became my friends. God uses these experiences to further our purpose. When things didn't work out, I could have gotten bitter or mad at these guys for not making something happen. However, what I didn't realize—and perhaps, they didn't realize—is that God was laying a foundation to build on. Later on, when I became the assistant director and coach at Faith West, I called upon Willie, Reggie, and Sweet Lou to do a Globetrotter exhibition against our coaching staff to raise money for our athletic program. Also, when I got my first college coaching job, one of my first recruits was Willie Foreman's nephew, Spencer Foreman. Spencer was one of my three first recruits at Palm Beach Atlantic University. Spencer became a leader and a good player for our program.

I must admit, I was a little confused as to what was next for me. I earned a degree in psychology with a concentration in counseling, but wasn't quite sure what to do with that my degree once I came to grips with the fact that the ride was over as far as trying to play professional basketball. My first job out of college was a good job with good pay. I was a house parent at a Behavior Training Institute. My responsibilities were to be the parent of three kids who suffered from autism, mental and emotional deficiencies, ADHD, etc. It was a very rewarding job. I had the opportunity to make a difference in young people's lives. There were several other duties that came with the job, such as cooking and feeding the kids, bussing them to school, and serving as a teacher. There were many challenges with this job, so we had to go through an extensive training program before we were released to work. The most difficult part of the job was having to be a part of restraining patients that were out of control. The other thing was I didn't like to see the kids so heavily medicated. However, we had to abide by the guidelines set by the MHMR standards of procedures. The job took a mental and emotional strain on the staff, which was why the job was four days on and four days off. That was much-needed time to recuperate from the taxing days on the job.

I learned so much from this experience and fell in love with many of the patients. I began to get a vision for the job: I wanted to do something to help rehabilitate them. A few of us approached the owner of the facility about a temporary release program, whereby the patients with good behavior could be released with supervision for a few hours of the day. This reward would give them some incentive to improve their behavior and have a desire to learn. The program was approved, so we were able to take kids to Rice football games, movies, bowling, and even to church. This became a ministry for me, and no longer a job. It was, by far, one of the most rewarding things I have done in my life. To take kids off campus and see the smile on their faces and the joy they had while being off campus was so satisfying. I began to accept that, perhaps, this was what God had in store for me. However, rumors started circulating that there was going to be a layoff of staff members. Just as I began to get comfortable and content with the job, I found out I was going to be laid off, because I was one of the last people hired. After about six months on the job, the company made changes, and I was released.

I was now back to a place of confusion and questioning my future and my purpose. Not to mention, I was engaged to be married, and now, I had no job. The one thing I knew was God did not bring me this far to turn back now. I put my faith and trust in God and began to just seek Him and serve Him in any capacity I could.

16

BACK TO THE HARDWOOD NOW AS A "COACH": A NAME CHANGING EXPERIENCE

In 1993, I was approached by my high school principal, Rick Tankersley, after a church service. He proceeded to tell me about the progress of Houston Christian Prep, which had changed its name to Faith West Academy. The school was in a major transition. After I graduated, the school went through many changes. There was no longer a high school, just elementary and junior high, but they were getting ready to make the move to reestablish a high school. So, he asked me if I would be interested in building the school a successful athletic program. He further explained that he would like for me to teach and coach. At this time in my life, I was in transition myself, trying to figure out what God had next for me. After a couple weeks of Rick calling to see what my interest was, I finally agreed to give it a shot. My hesitation was because I never thought of myself as a coach, much less an athletic director and teacher. Furthermore, I have to be honest and say, I had always thought I would be doing something on a much higher level, paying a lot more money. As I mentioned earlier, the offer was to be the athletic director and coach, and teach history, math, and P.E.—all of these responsibilities for a whopping $18,000. This was a huge pay cut from my first job, and it came with more responsibilities.

You see, people sometimes live their life for a job. When you are in search of your purpose in life, it doesn't always start with the biggest paycheck, nor all the bells and whistles.

God has a bigger purpose in starting your journey to discovering His purpose. "God's ways are not our ways, neither are His thoughts like ours, as high as the heavens are from the earth, so are His ways from ours" (Isaiah 55:9).

Now, I'm not saying that for some people, their beginning journey will not or won't begin with a nice paycheck or extreme blessings. Each person's purpose is different. It is usually based on the amount of impact God has called for your purpose. Obviously, for me, coaching was an opportunity to impact the lives of young people and their families. I have been honored to be a part of the many people's lives God placed in my life.

17

MY COACHING CAREER BEGINS

Some things we do in life do not come with a manuscript. For me, I had never been a teacher, coach, or even an athletic director, but the experiences we have prepare us in ways we never know until we are put to the test. The greatest challenge in any building situation is finances. The school did not have any funds to buy any equipment, uniforms, basketballs etc. You can imagine the pressure I felt on a new job. Then, on top of that, the student athletes that came out for tryouts had no clue of what basketball was all about. You take a guy like me—who was passionate about and loved the game and was somewhat of an accomplished player—having to coach kids who had no desire or knowledge of it at all. I often thought to myself, "What have I gotten myself into?" But as in almost everything I faced in life, I took it as a challenge and began to build from scratch. So, I took a group of ninth graders and began a journey of building a championship program.

Because the school did not have any money, I had no money to hire coaches. So, any sport I wanted to start, guess who was the coach? Yep, you got it! I coached the boys' and girls' junior high and high school basketball, track, flag football, and volleyball. I was blessed in my efforts to raise money to buy balls, uniforms, and some other equipment for all sports. I was on my way—except now, it was time for the games! That's when reality hit. We got beat in every sport very badly. I had never experienced such defeat before in my life. The one thing I have experienced was the **dedication, commitment, confidence, work ethic, discipline, patience, fortitude, perseverance, good attitude, and teamwork to bounce back, keep trying, and never give up!** These were the lessons I begin to instill in these kids—but most of all, **to Honor God in everything we do**—and I promised them if we kept working hard and committed ourselves to being the best, sooner than later, we would be the best!

Needless to say, we fell short on most nights we competed in each sport! I have to give these kids credit: they took every word I said and began to believe we could be the best! I knew if I was going to be successful, I needed help. So, I raised enough money and convinced the administration to start hiring teachers who could also coach. We began to build a staff who could take some responsibilities off of me. My biggest hire was my best friend, Demaris Ray, from college who lived in Philadelphia, Pennsylvania. He decided to relocate and take over the track program, as he had run track in college. Demaris also assisted me in basketball and football. I was also able to hire volleyball coaches. I began to see the light of all the possibilities Faith West Academy could be. **My goal was to build the most successful athletic program that embodied Christian character, community service, and academic achievement.**

18

TOUCHED BY A LEGEND: "PISTOL PETE MARAVICH"

The first thing I did to ensure growth in the athletes was start my very own **Reaching New Heights Basketball Camp**—one that reflected the only camp I had ever experienced with Pistol Pete Maravich. I ran a camp that enforced character over athletics, teamwork, and hard work. The most significant thing was closing out camp with a message to change young people's lives. Camp was a huge success, the most rewarding thing I have had the pleasure to be a part of.

The first year, we competed as an independent team! In my second year, we joined the Texas Christian Athletic League, which was a statewide organization that allowed for small Christian schools to compete for state championships. My kids made me very proud. In just our second year of competing, we had a winning season. We only lost the regionals in volleyball, but in girls' and boys' basketball, we won the regionals and advanced to the state championships. In track, we won regionals and advanced to state, and to top it off, our junior high girls and boys won their conference championships. Faith West became a talked-about school in just a short time. Many athletes from the community and other schools began to gain interest in attending this small, Christian school. But as in all things, with growth comes more challenges, more finances, and the need for more coaches, uniforms, and equipment. My job was becoming more and more challenging, because let's not forget, I was still teaching six classes—Bible, history, and physical education. This was a job that required me to find strength in another source: God! I can remember many days and nights spent praying for strength, guidance, and resources.

Year three, we took another step in building a successful program. We joined a much more recognizable and competitive league, called the Texas Association of Private and Parochial Schools (TAPPS). This organization forced us to play much larger private schools and even bigger public schools. Our kids responded to the challenge very well, winning district and conference championships before losing in regionals. The school was even better. Every sport was successful, and we were finally headed into the final year of completing the high school transition. We now had seniors who understood what it took to win and play together as a team and work hard. Over the summer, there was a relentless effort on the kids' parts to get better. Everyone showed up to basketball camp and even traveled to other camps. Demaris and I started a next level camp that included more strength, conditioning, and agility drills. Not only did our kids show up, but camp was a huge community success. This gave us more notoriety and visibility, and students again wanted to be a part of a growing, successful program.

Year four came around, and now that we had seniors, the school needed a high school counselor. And guess who that was— yep. Me. Now I'm a teacher and coach of many teams, athletic director, and a counselor. I was able to cut back on some teaching duties. As a counselor, I was very proud to learn that three of my athletes were in the running for valedictorian and salutatorian. Once again, we had tremendous success as an athletic program, competing in TAPPS and excelling! Volleyball and our boys' basketball lost in regionals, but our girls' basketball team made it to the state championship game. This was huge accomplishment for the school. All of the school bussed to Waco, Texas from Katy to support what could be the school's first state championship! I was so excited to be a part of my alma mater, and how far the school, and those kids, had gone!

Well, we got it done. Faith West Academy won its first-ever state championship. It was a very proud moment for me. I imagine the feeling was even better than playing in the NBA. Our track team finished the year by also competing for a state championship but fell short. Oh, did I mention I started a baseball team, and they also advanced to the playoffs? The transition was complete for now, but we do live in Texas, where football is king. This would be the next sport on my agenda to start, and then, soccer. Well, you can imagine how much money it takes to start a football program, so I was not able to start football. But I did start the soccer program. We were off and running!

19

THE BLESSED AND HAPPY YEARS

Now that we had a full-fledge high school, it was my responsibility to take each program to a championship level! Our girls' basketball team had achieved that honor, and now, it was the goal for each program. The following year, each team had experienced the same—if not better—success. The only difference was the girls lost in the state championship game. The girls went on to compete in four more state championships. It was a tremendous privilege that in two of those years, I had the opportunity to coach the girls and boys in back-to-back games in the state championship. Each program maintains a high level of competition year in and year out, right on the cusp of competing for state or regional championships.

Now, it was time for football. I had finally raised enough money to buy equipment and uniforms. We had the luxury in the state of Texas of starting a six-man program, instead of eleven! In our first year as a six-man program, we finished the season ranked second in the state. Unfortunately, we could not compete for the state championship, being a first-year program. After the first year, we progressed to eleven-man football, but we could not compete for the state title. In our first year as a full member to compete for the state title, we had everyone returning from the previous season, plus we added a few studs who had transferred in. We put a schedule in place that would allow for us to be prepared for a state championship run. What we didn't take into consideration was the mental make-up of the team. We started the season one to three, with our only win being against an inferior opponent. Our most recent defeat was a blowout, and the players were very discouraged. After the ballgame, it was "D time". This was decision-making time. We were either going to fold up the tent or pull together and work harder than ever to become champions. There was a lot of speculation on why the basketball coach was coaching the football team. Many people around the state criticized my ability to coach football, but I had played football in my younger years— I knew how to lead, demand hard work, and motivate a group of young men. I assembled a staff that specialized in the things I did not know. I was an offensive player, so I understood offense. Needless to say, this meeting on the field after the game lasted until the lights were turned off.

I told each parent they must wait until the meeting was over before anyone could leave. I needed to know that night who was with me and who was not. So, I drew a line in the sand and said, "Whoever is committed to giving their heart and soul to this team and program, step across the line." One by one, with tears in their eyes, everyone stepped across the line. The players began hugging each other and encouraging one another. It was a scene I will never forget. There we were, on the visiting field, having an unbelievably life-changing moment. I told our coaching staff that meant us, too. It was time we all gave our very best efforts to get the most out of this team and honor God with our talents. We huddled up, prayed, and committed the rest of the season to God and each other. The next game, we were playing a very good program and the previous state champions; we won that game 63 to 0. Each game we got better and better, blowing every opponent out.

Soon, it was time to face a coach who had dominated the district and had won many state titles. He also was my biggest critic about being a basketball coach trying to coach football. We were on a six-game winning streak, so our guys were pumped and ready to go. We dominated every phase of the game and won 61 to 6 on their field. We celebrated by winning the district championship and had the opportunity to make a run at state. We caught a break in the first round. The school we were supposed to play had been found playing illegal players, so we advanced to the second round! Since we were the highest seeded team, we got to host the next game. We went on to win that game 48 to 20. The school was so excited, and there was a lot of excitement in the community. Here we were, a small private school, that only had 20 players. After injuries and academically ineligible players, we found ourselves with a lot of two-way players. Next were the semi-finals, and we had to go on the road and play another well-established program six hours away. Their coach had 20-plus years experience coaching football, and again, the critics came out, saying, "They won't beat this team; that coach is going to out coach them." They were wrong. We won the ball game 26 to 0, in rain and mud, on their field. We were headed to the state championship in the first year we were able to compete! The players, school family, and city were all so excited. It was a red, blue, and white week! Everyone was making plans to see the Faith West Academy Eagles compete for the state championship in Waco, Texas at Baylor University—a huge stadium for our small Christian school and fans.

Well, the game was here. We had made it to the biggest game, the grandest stage for high school football, especially in Texas. We went into the game averaging 56 points a game, so we were on a torrid pace of scoring. But this was the state championship, and both teams were well scouted and prepared. My guys started out nervous, making unusual plays, fumbling the ball, penalties, and throwing interceptions. We had three touchdowns called back, and we found ourselves down 6 to 0 after the first quarter. They scored on a freak play where there was a deflection, and the ball popped in the air. One of their players caught it and ran in for a touchdown. I saw a similar look in the guy's eyes when we were on a losing streak. I called the guys together and told them we had to pull together and concentrate. They were not better than we were, and we were beating ourselves. Then, I told them to remember "D time". We were destined to be the champs.

We went out and drove straight down the field and took the lead, 7 to 6, and it would remain that way at halftime. We made adjustments at halftime, but it was more of the same results. We were just not ourselves, offensively. It was the fourth quarter, and I knew if we could score one more touchdown, we would be able to put the game away. Since we were not sharp on offense, we turned to our defense to preserve the victory, and they were doing a fantastic job. The opposing team was thinking the same way, so it was a matter of who would throw the knockout punch. O'Connell punted the ball to us, and the ball went over my punt returners' head and rolled to the one-yard line. There was about six minutes on the clock, and we were in the worst position possible. I called our "O line" together and told them if we were going to win this game, it was going to be them leading the way. We needed to drive that ball down the field, and put this game away.

On the first play, we handed the ball off, and "boom"— right through a gaping hole, my running back took off for a 50-plus-yard run. The crowd went wild, and I finally saw the team that had had so much confidence going into the game. Our line responded, and from that point on, we ran the ball down their throats until we finally scored a huge touchdown. The only thing was we scored so quickly, the opposing team had a chance to tie the ball game, because we had missed the extra point. We were winning 13 to 6, and it was up to the defense to bring us home. Our defense stepped up and shut the opposing team down, and they turned the ball over to us and we had only one thing to do: take a knee and run the clock out. In 2000, Faith West Academy won the state championship in its first year of competition, and with a basketball coach leading the way. It was one of the most satisfying moments of my life, taking a group of guys who did not know how to win, bringing them together on one specific night "D time", and leading them to a championship in the same year I was able to lead the basketball team to state, as well.

After many years of success and having built a highly accomplished athletic program, there was a change in the administration. The new administration and I did not share the same philosophy. They wanted to make many changes regarding athletics, and I was personally tired of coaching all the teams. I went to the administration and asked to step down from a couple of sports, and their response was not good. I was crushed, but thought it was time to move on, and I did! I spent eight years at my alma mater, and I was very proud and blessed to have been a part of building a successful athletic program and developing a counseling department, and I was most proud to have played a part in many young people's lives being changed. Also, the kids got the message academically, for each year I was there, one of my athletes was valedictorian or salutatorian.

20

THE NEXT LEVEL

The way my life was going, I thought I was rotating around in a circle! In 2002, Liberty University was at the bottom of NCAA Division One Basketball. They decided to hire one of the assistant coaches who was on staff when I was a player as the head coach—Randy Dunton! Randy called me and proposed to me the opportunity to come back to Liberty as an assistant coach and help rebuild a championship level program. For me, Liberty was the place where I learned the value of hard work, teamwork, and character. As you can imagine, I was excited to be able to go back and build a winning program. My job was as the assistant coach and recruiting coordinator. It was my responsibility to bring in the kind of players who would represent Liberty in character, academics, and competition! This was a major responsibility, and one I did not take lightly! I immediately put all my time and energy into learning the ropes and figuring out how to get the edge on the competition. The obvious place for me to start was to recruit players around the country who reflected the values of the university and recruit the places where I knew a lot of players: Texas.

The first year, we had a good season, finishing second in the conference, and we signed a top-60 recruiting class in the country. This was huge, because there were over 300 schools across the country. We signed some very good players who we felt could take us to the next level. The second year came, and we had high expectations. We started the year 3 to 8, and there was a lot of speculation on whether or not our coaching staff was capable of doing the job. Also, there was pressure on me, because I had brought in players who were not playing well. We were entering the conference play and went on the road and lost to the last-place team. We went on to the next game and lost again. By this time, we were falling apart; the players were discouraged, and the coaches were spinning their heads, trying to figure out what in the world was going on. The seniors' captains came to me in the restaurant on the way home and expressed some feelings that needed to be addressed. I went to the head coach and told him we needed to look at this situation and make some changes. Obviously, the responsibility was on the players to play better, and that's just what they decided to do. After the players had a long productive meeting with the head coach, they responded. We had five of the next seven games at home, so this was the perfect time to build some momentum and get the fans excited again. Needless to say, we went out and won 15 of the next 18 games, including the regular-season championship and the conference championship. We had done it: Liberty was back on the map and out of the cellar dweller.

We advanced to the NCAA Tournament for only the second time in school history. There was mad chaos on campus and in the community; everyone was so excited for our players and program. As for me, it was a tremendous moment for me to once again return to my alma mater and play a part of making them a winner. We were selected to go to Buffalo and take on top seeded St. Joe's University, who had had an incredible year. Ranked number one in the nation throughout the year, we had our work cut out for us. This was a terrific experience; one I will never forget.

We lost that first-round game to St. Joe's, but things were looking up, and as we were returning, we had another successful recruiting class, this time ranked in the top 50. Liberty University, a small Christian University, was making national headline news and building a reputation.

Year three came around, and again, we had a very good team returning—arguably our two best players was returning, who were only freshmen, along with experienced and good players who would provide leadership. Also, we had signed another good recruiting class, plus we had two top prospects sitting out: one had transferred from the University of Houston, and the other was a Prop 48 top prospect, who had had to sit out the first year. What was supposed to be a great season and a repeat of conference champions and another trip to the NCAA tournament, was met with many challenges. Although we were very talented, our team chemistry and discipline suffered. We had discipline issues with a few players and a disjointed group, which when we pulled them together, we were still successful. However, when faced with adversity, we just could not pull things together. Although we still had a good season, we fell short and finished second in the conference and were devastated when we lost in the conference semi-finals. But again, things were looking up, because we only lost one player, and signed another top-70 recruiting class.

However, it was important to me that we get back to the foundation of what Liberty was all about. So, I wanted to make sure there was a commitment to proper process to success. My off-season was met with many challenges that began to cloud my vision of where I was. My wife's father passed away back in Houston. So, we went to attend the service and funeral. It is often said when God takes a life, He gives a life. For a brief moment, my wife and I thought that was the case. While we were in Houston, we found out she was pregnant. What was a sad and difficult time in our life turn into joyful experience. How awesome, because we had tried and tried many times to get pregnant and had been unsuccessful, so this was a wonderful blessing. Unfortunately, this joyful experience was short-lived. While sleeping, my wife felt something was not right, got up to use the restroom, and felt something drop into the toilet. In that moment, we were shockingly afraid she may have had a miscarriage. So, the next morning, it was confirmed she had, indeed, had a miscarriage. However, the doctor gave us some good news. Although we had miscarried, there was still a detection of another fetus, so we were still pregnant and expecting our first child.

As you can imagine, this was a very difficult and an emotional rollercoaster. So, because my wife was pregnant, she wanted to be close to family to go through the pregnancy. We began to discuss returning home— after all, I was experiencing some challenges at Liberty that were concerning, but we were doing well in so many ways. Liberty was the place where I had cut my teeth as a person, a player, and a coach. The most difficult thing was to leave all the players I had played a major role in recruiting. I was faced with a very difficult decision. After returning home to lay my wife's father to rest, we first needed to find a good OB/GYN to set an appointment to know the status of the baby. What was supposed to be a joyous, exciting doctor's appointment turned into another devastating moment. After exams and mammograms, the doctor told us she had some difficult news to share with us. In a sigh of grief and concern, she said, "I'm so sorry to tell you, but you have a tubular pregnancy, or ectopic pregnancy." This occurs when a fertilized egg implants and grows outside the main cavity of the uterus. In other words, the fertilized eggs cannot survive outside the uterus.

When you receive news like this, as a Christian, your thoughts move in many different directions. Obviously, the first emotion is devastation, but as a man, you are forced to be strong and encourage your wife. We were so overwhelmed that our first response to the doctor was what does this mean, and of course, she replied, "You're going to have to terminate the pregnancy." Again, in a Christian response, we thought that God could do a miracle. However, after many discussions about the process of what would happen to the baby, we had no choice but to accept that the pregnancy had to be terminated. We left the doctor's office completely devastated. Talk about being in a state of confusion and disappointment. We had just returned from laying my father-in-law to rest, we had miscarried a child, and now we had to terminate the other child, and I was unsure of whether I should return to Liberty for another season.

My first responsibility was to do what was best in regards to my wife, and put my career on hold. At this time, being a coach was the last thing on my mind. My wife and I consulted with family and mentors, fasted and prayed about what should we do. They told us to set an appointment for the termination process, and we were struggling with this idea of going through the procedures. After exhausting days of thoughts prayers and communication, we called and set a date to go forward with the procedure. Meanwhile, I had agreed that I would resign from Liberty, which was very difficult, as well, and allow God to lead me wherever my next step was. What I was sure about was that I would still like to coach, I just had no idea where. This was a complete step of faith. Scripture tells us in Hebrews 11:1, "Now faith is the substance of things hope for the evidence of things not seen." The goal was to head back to Houston, but I left it up to God. I thought if God wanted me to continue to be a coach, He would work things out.

21

TIME TO MOVE ON

A fter I made the decision to resign, I was faced with a difficult decision. I love Liberty University, no better place to be in the world, and after all the university had done for me, it was tough to let go. Even though when I took the job, I did so by taking a pay cut, it was my alma mater, so I felt honored to be a part of rebuilding the basketball program, and even though it was not the best job financially, it was definitely the most rewarding. Before I left Liberty, there were a couple of people to whom I felt I owed a great deal of gratitude: Dr. Jerry Falwell—

founder and chancellor of the university—and Kim Graham, who was the assistant director. I met with both gentlemen before I left, and they were gracious in accepting my resignation, and even honored my salary until June, giving me a few months to find another job. I conveyed my heartfelt gratitude for the opportunity to come back to the place where it all began for me as a Christian, student athlete. I began to embrace the idea of a change. It seemed like it was the perfect time to do something different. Furthermore, I had a desire to be a head coach again.

One day, I was sitting at my desk in the office, and I got a blind email that basically said, "Would you be interested in being the head basketball coach at Palm Beach Atlantic University?" I thought, "Wow, is this to me?" So, I looked at the school online and checked out the qualifications, and sure enough, the job was open. As you can imagine, I looked around the room, thinking "God, are you here?" I was excited and confused at the same time. But I thought I should go ahead and fill out the application. The very next day, I received an email of confirmation from the committee on my application, and a question of if I would be available later on for a phone interview. I quickly responded yes and was anxious the rest of the day, until the time had come for the interview. I had spent the whole day preparing myself with all the information I needed to be able to answer each question. There was no way I was going to blow this interview.

The interview went really well, and then, it was time to decide on a time to visit the university campus and meet everyone. This was a very exciting moment, but there was one problem: how could I possibly convince my wife that instead of going home, we should move to South Florida and have a new outlook on life. As you could imagine, my wife was still grieving and really desired to move back home. However, when I explained the opportunity and possibilities, she agreed to at least take a visit. I was excited, and God smiled on us and our situation. He proved Himself to be faithful.

My visit to the campus was unbelievable. After all, this private, Christian university was in West Palm Beach, Florida—one of America's most beautiful, extravagant cities. The facility was nice, and so were the people; they were making the move to NCAA Division Two, another chance for me to build a foundation of a winning program, and I would get to do it at a Christian university. The only thing left to do was negotiate a contract and make a decision. After days of negotiating, my wife and I decided to accept the opportunity. The only thing now was I had to tell all the players, recruits, and their families—which was going to be hard. I made the tough decision and decided to move on from Liberty!

22

THE TOUGH YEARS

For all its beauty and splendor, it was difficult to make ends meet in West Palm Beach, and when I got to the university, the struggles financially did not allow me to recruit the way I was used to. I began to think it was going to be a challenge! I began getting out in the community and raising money, creating awareness—I even called upon help from Dr. Jerry Falwell. I called Jerry and asked if there were any financially heavy hitters in the area he knew and didn't mind passing on to me. He gladly gave me some contacts to pursue. I chopped down as many trees as possible to raise support for the program, and thankfully, God did send a few people my way. Since scholarship and budget money was low, I decided to build from the bottom and bring in a class of freshmen. I groomed them to be ready to win in a couple of years. On the court was a struggle, as we just didn't have the horses to compete with well-established programs. We had a few big wins, and played many close games, but this situation was going to require lots of patience. I was so used to jumping into new situations and having success.

Year two was about the same as the first year: we lost most of our games by less than five points. We were getting close and needed just a little help from the school. I approached the university administration, who had expressed tremendous satisfaction with the direction of the program, especially with all the campus and community excitement there was surrounding it. Although we were not winning games, our kids were playing hard, serving in the community, and building campus spirit. There were a lot of positive things happening, and I was proud of what we had done so far. My meeting with the administration was positive, and I was filled with a lot of hope, until I was called into a meeting with the assistant director, who told me there was going to be a budget cut. My heart sank. I had spent two years putting this program in a position to win, and we were headed in the wrong direction. Also, I was told that I would not be getting a raise, as I had been promised. I was devastated, and so were my players! The only thing I knew to do was to pray and trust God, so that's exactly what I did. After a couple weeks of praying and thinking, I received another email. This time, it was from a former colleague at Palm Beach Atlantic who had gone on to get an athletic director job in South Texas. After a couple of conversations and a visit to the campus, I accepted a job at Texas A&M International University!

23

BACK TO TEXAS

A fter speaking with the president about the opportunity, I expressed that I would love to take the challenge of building a nationally competitive program. The next day, I resigned from Palm Beach Atlantic and began to set my sights on returning to my home state of Texas. My first goal was to make sure the budgets were good enough to build something special and make the funds available for those players who were at Palm Beach who might want to transfer. I had promised them I would take care of them by the time they were juniors! All the meetings and visits went well, so I was off to Laredo, Texas—a border town just nine miles from Mexico! New job, new opportunity, and the challenges for this job were trifold. In previous years, the players had displayed poor academic achievement, poor judgement and character, and a lack of winning on the court.

As in all situations, my first task was to make sure we had quality young men in the program, ones who embodied what being a true athlete was all about: character, academic performance, hard work, and teamwork. This was also a transition to NCAA Division Two, and therefore, we were not eligible to compete for the conference championship. That made this situation even more difficult, keeping a group of young men focused on improving the program without a reward. But my message was clear: the reward was laying a championship foundation, reaching the community, and building campus spirit. We had a great first year, and we reached out to the community in many ways, putting on events to connect with the student body and community, serving in the community, speaking at public school functions, fundraising, and hosting camps. Most of my players had made commitments to attend church as a team, and I felt really good about our future. We were headed in the right direction on the court, we had several big wins, and we finished middle of the pack in conference. We had the core nucleus coming back, including two players who had made all conference, along with our four other top scorers. Finally, exciting things were happening for me. I had not experienced losing like the past few years, and I was really being tested.

The week before school started, I was in my office working, and I received a call from the trainer, who told me Chris Swan was crying in the training room and was in severe pain! I rushed over to the training room and found my leading scorer and all conference player, laying on the table with his leg trembling and twitching so much, he could not stop it. The trainer explained that Chris had tripped and felt something pop in his knee. I knew that feeling. Chris Swan had torn his ACL, MCL, and LCL, had total knee damage, plus he had damaged his nerve. As any coach would do, I focused on the kid, kept his spirit up, contacted the team, and comforted them. But this was a tremendous blow to our team for the upcoming year. The year began, and we duplicated the off-season impact, plus we put on a monumental cross-border event. I was able to negotiate with the Mexican professional team to play us in an exhibition game. It was a huge success in every way, so we were off to a good start, despite the adversity we were facing. On the court, we started the winning against the 13th ranked team in the country! Everything looked positive, until the injury bug hit us again. Our top prospect and center was out indefinitely with back pains, and one other top recruit was out with a knee injury! As much as we had worked hard to build something special, it all seemed to be falling apart. We had an injury-plagued season, along with academic issues. The season was a huge disappointment to me and my players. But to the fans, administration, and community, they were still excited about the direction we were headed in.

24

HOW TO HANDLE A STORM

Folks, let me tell you, storms in our life are inevitable. Whether we choose the storm, or the storms choose us. Tough times are God's way of getting us to grow and to trust Him more. Also, we go through these times because God is refining us through allowing us to see our strengths and discovering our weaknesses. In 2009, there was a tremendous amount of excitement in the TAMIU basketball program. My coaching staff and I worked really hard in the off-season, and we brought in what we thought was a really good recruiting class. We were now a somewhat household name in the community, whereby the wealthy gentleman made a huge donation to the university and athletic program, as well as donated scholarships for the basketball program.

Things were looking up, until I got a phone call from our athletic director. Each year as a college basketball coach, I tried to attend the NCAA final four for the purpose of attending classes to gain knowledge, network, and build relationships. While I was in Detroit at the final four in 2009, I received a call from the athletic director, who notified me that we needed to meet when I returned. Upon my return, I had a meeting with the athletic director and the NCAA representative, and they informed me that the conference had called them to look into a possible player cheating to be eligible. I was shocked that to hear the news, but my response was I had zero knowledge of any player cheating to gain eligibility. I was notified they would be doing an in-house investigation into the possibility. I told them to let me know if there was anything I could do to get to the bottom of the accusations. I told them I was going to have a team meeting to address the issue and see if anyone came forward.

After a day or so went by, I was called into the athletic director's office, where I was informed that they had not found anyone responsible. However, they would continue to look into the situation and let me know what they found. Later that evening, I received a call from the athletic director that I needed to be in a meeting with the president first thing in the morning. The very next day, I got up and went to meet with the president, and as I walked into the conference room, I noticed that there were several attendees. I became concerned about what had happened. The meeting that took place was to reveal that the university had found players on my team who were guilty of a cheating scandal. I was asked several questions as to my knowledge of the situation, to which I emphatically denied any knowledge of any kid or player cheating. It was a lengthy conversation, which lasted a couple hours, and once they were done with questioning me, I was allowed to leave. I went to my office, called my assistant coaches in the room, and informed them of the findings and the possibility of punishment.

While I was sitting in my office, I received a phone call from the president's office, informing me I had been put on a temporary leave of absence until they got to the bottom of this cheating scandal. I was completely devastated and somewhat insulted that my name would be confused with anyone who might cheat to get eligible. I was a coach who held my players to a high standard academically. As soon as I had arrived on the campus, with the help of the AD I started a study hall program for the university, to ensure student athletes would perform as well as normal student. Furthermore, we lost to the number one team in the country that year, because I had suspended my second leading scorer, because he did not meet our team GPA. This came as a complete shock and devastating blow to my character and my profession. I could not help but think why would God allow something to happen of this magnitude, when I had worked so hard and put so much work into doing things the right way, holding kids to a high standard and competing at the highest levels to build a championship program.

I was in complete shock and confused as to what should I do. I called my mom and dad and told them what had happened, and as they have always been supportive and encouraging, they encouraged me to hang in there and let the process play itself out and prayed with me that God would cover me in the midst of this situation. It was a very lonely time for me, because just a few months before this, I had gotten into a car accident where I had hit two cows on a country backroad and spun off the road about 100 yards onto the median. I had crawled out unscathed, so I knew that God had a purpose for my life for me to have escaped that accident. However, upon going to the doctor, I learned that I had so much stress, I was not swallowing properly. I was throwing up almost every day and could not hold food down. I had to take a lot of tests, and they even thought I had cancer at one point. The year I had thought was going to be something great had turned into the most tumultuous, most challenging year of my life. Between 2008 and 2009, I was going through a divorce, my job was being threatened and taken from me, my health was attacked, and I found myself alone, asking God why I must go through this. I began to wonder what I was going to do with my life, as I had spent the past 15 years coaching—using my talents, my gifts, and my testimony to impact the lives of young people through this great game of basketball. There I was, on the verge of losing my career, the only thing I had known since I had graduated from college.

After a few days went by, I was finally called back into the president's office, and he informed me I had a choice to either resign or be let go. I asked the president what I had done to lose my job. I had zero knowledge of any kid cheating on any test or doing anything to be eligible. The president and I had a heartfelt emotional conversation, and he told me I had had kids under my watch who had participated in a cheating scandal that went back several years. He told me there was nothing he could do to save my job, even though he had respected and appreciated all the work I had done in the two short years I had been in Laredo. I was completely devastated, broken, and shattered beyond belief that I could no longer coach. Unashamed, the tears began to fall, and I was completely disappointed. I called Dave and Lynne again, who tried their very best to comfort me and encourage me. However, there was nothing anyone could say at that point and time, because the profession I loved was gone. After consulting my college coach and a few other coaches in the profession— like my old friends Jerome Tang and Mike Davis, who was coaching at University of Indiana. I was advised I should fight for my job. I spent day and night, weeping and not knowing what to do, and asking God to give me a favor in this situation.

I woke up one day, and it occurred to me they could take coaching from me, but they couldn't take my name. I was an inner-city kid who had been given a second chance in life, who had made the most of the opportunity through hard work and perseverance, I had built successful career in coaching basketball and established a good name in every community. I determined that day that there was no way I was going to go quietly and allow them to ruin my name, when I had absolutely zero knowledge of what the players and athletes did to gain eligibility.

I got some information from a really good friend of mine, who put me in touch with a lawyer back in Houston, Charles Peckham. I had heard he had served on a case for another college coach in a similar situation. I reached out to Charles, and I'll be forever and eternally grateful for him and his friendship. Charles and I spent a lot of time on the phone reviewing and going over the situation as I knew it, and then, he made his way to Laredo and did an investigation into the situation. He concluded there was no way my name should be tied to the situation. Therefore, he asked me what did I want to do? I told him it was important for me to clear my name, because I had worked my whole life to build a good name, and my reputation meant everything to me. At first, I stated I wanted my job back, because I did not know how to let go of being a coach. The very thing I had fallen in love with and enjoyed doing was seemingly out of the question. Charles told me he would do whatever I wanted to do, but I said I just wanted my name cleared.

So, we met with the president and the lawyers of the Texas A&M system to do an internal investigation. The Texas A&M system hired their own group to look into the situation, and they concluded that myself and others had no role or knowledge in the cheating scandal. However, because of all of the mudslinging going on through the process, it was best that I resign. My name was cleared, and the president wrote me a letter of recommendation. It was a triumphant day in some aspects, and before the meeting was concluded, Charles Peckham asked the group if he could read them something? Charles read a letter that spoke of a man with good character, a hardworking attitude, and respect, love, and care for people and the community. I was unaware of this letter, but Charles concluded by asking, "Is this the kind of person you guys will be looking to hire to replace my client?" Without hesitation, the committee responded in an emphatic yes. Charles replied, "These are the words your president used to describe the man you are letting go."

In one fell swoop, a peace and contentment came over me. It was a devastating blow to my life. After all, I was all alone in Laredo, with no real direction. Like in everything I did, I always sought the guidance of Dave and Lynne Johnson, who told me I needed to pack my bags and come home and regroup. They encouraged me that God would restore all that had been taken from me one day. For the first time in my life since graduating from college, I felt lost, confused, and hurt beyond repair. I question whether coaching was for me. But the funny thing is no matter what I have done in my life, there's only one thing that people call me. They call me Coach!

25

NEW DIRECTION

I once heard a slogan that in order to become what God wants you to become, you have to endure adversity. It is His desire to make you stronger in the struggle to prepare you for the next level in your journey. Upon returning home, I came in contact with a really good friend, Tony Dutt. He was an NBA agent, and he noticed my talent and tried to create opportunities for me to play professional basketball. At that time, Tony was a football and basketball agent, and he asked me what I was doing with myself. We had stayed in touch over the years, so he knew I was a college basketball coach, but I told him I was actually free and looking for another opportunity. Tony and I had always discussed that I would work for him one day, and lo and behold, Tony offered me the opportunity to be a part of his agency, Dutt Sports Services, where I could be in charge of training marketing for players and recruiting. It was an exciting opportunity for me. It kept me in the game of basketball and gave me a new challenge that I could learn and grow from. Tony took me underneath his wings and showed me the world of sports agents. He introduced me to clients he currently had in the NBA, and as God would have it, I knew a few of them already from high school, in my time of recruiting as a college coach. So, I was excited about a new direction in life.

I begin to discover my love and passion for training. I recall one specific situation in which Tony told me that there was a 7'5" kid from Senegal coming to Houston, and the Dallas Mavericks wanted to bring him to camp. He asked me if I could train the kid to get him ready for camp. It was an exciting opportunity for me to have my own project as a player to get him ready for the NBA. I began studying techniques and concepts and reflected on the things I had learned over the years, dating back to the time where I had been injured in college, and Coach Jeff Meyer asked me to serve as student assistant coach where I would help with training and skill development. God does not make mistakes, although it was devastating to not be able to play my senior year. I began training the 7'5" young man and saw tremendous progress with him within two weeks, since we had to get him ready for the Dallas Mavericks. The key to being a successful agent is to be able to sign players who are under contract where you can receive a percentage of the salary. That was a difficult challenge for me, so my time as an agent in training was cut short, because I missed out on signing guys who could produce money.

I am grateful to Tony Dutt, who gave me the opportunity, for I learned a great deal, but I also found a new direction as a trainer. While I was in transition from working with Tony full-time, I received a phone call from Faith West Academy. They had just lost a basketball coach and wanted to know if I was available to step in and coach the team. I was in a bit of a transition, so I decided to take the job and try and help the school get the basketball program back to being a state championship contender. My return to Faith West was a bit more of a difficult challenge, as many of the private schools had advanced in their ability to recruit top prospects and become more dedicated to their sports programs. Faith West was behind in that aspect, and the philosophy and leadership structure was different than what I had experienced when I had first built the athletic program in 1993. However, as in all things I have done in my life, I see difficult challenges as an opportunity to do something great. I began to build relationships with players and families, and I started doing training outside of school to make some extra money. My reconnection to the community began to be profitable, as I began to build the basketball program. We got a few good players to transfer into the school, and things were looking good.

However, I began to face opposition with the type of players we were inheriting. Because of this opposition, I met with the administration and expressed my concerns and opinions. The response to my concerns was met without any changes to allow me to be successful. So, I began to pour my time and energy into the training I was doing outside the program. It was shortly after that someone asked me why I didn't train full-time and start an AAU program. They told me there was a great need in the community for someone with my talent and experience, and people were paying lots of money for less than what I was doing for training. Faith West was near and dear to my heart. It is the place of my rebirthing experience and my foundation of who I became as a Christian. This was a very difficult decision. I prayed, fasted, and asked God for clarity, so I asked to meet with the administration, just to be clear what the plan and objectives were for the basketball program. I will never forget: we met at a Five Guys Burgers and Fries restaurant one afternoon for lunch. I once again expressed my concern, and this time, through my prayers and seeking God, I had a few other concerns. Needless to say, nothing changed, and after much thought and consideration, I resigned from Faith West. In 2011, I launched the Reaching New Heights Basketball and Training Program and Shooting Stars AAU team. It was through all of the adversity that I discovered a new path in life. and I now had a second profession. I wasn't just a coach, I had now officially become a trainer. But make no mistake about it, everyone still called me Coach.

26

REACHING NEW HEIGHTS AND SHOOTING STARS AAU IS LAUNCHED

As I looked back and calculated my journey, I realized God was teaching me many lessons. The jobs that were met with opposition are sometimes an act of God to move you on to other things. It doesn't take away the hurt or disappointment you experience along the way, but it gives you perspective. Hopefully, you are taking notes and learning from each failed experience. I learned that nothing great can be accomplished without proper leadership. It is a critical part of everyone's success. It's important who you work for, who you play for, and who you work with. Don't be afraid to make difficult decisions when you are faced with opposition. Sometimes, it is a sign that it is time to move on. I like to travel and drive a lot, and one of my biggest pet peeves is stopping and staying somewhere too long. It prevents you from ever reaching your destination in a timely manner, or you're worn out by the time you get there.

The pay from Faith West was so little that training was a way I could make some extra money, so I took on the opportunity to train this young man. Soon after that, his parent asked why I didn't start an AAU team, because they were not sure they were going back to the team her son had previously played on. So, I had a try out to see how many or how much interest there was in starting an AAU program. Little did I know, there was a lot of interest, so in 2011, I launched the Reaching New Heights Basketball AAU team. As I began to build the business, we started with three teams. This was a great foundation to build on, and along with training, it was enough to financially take care of my family at that time. Although the on-the-court experience wasn't the best for all the teams, it was the beginning of something special. One of the unique things was I was able to employ two of my former college players, Derek Barnes and Sean Tucker. These two guys were my first two recruits when I had gotten my first coaching job at Palm Beach Atlantic University. These two also followed me to Texas A&M International University and were my two leading scorers and all-conference players. It was great to put two successful college players in front of the AAU teams. I was also able to reunite with my assistant coach, Jared Goodwin, who had coached with me at Palm Beach Atlantic and Texas A&M International University. Jared had always balanced me and brought strengths that served the program well.

We were off and running. I laid out a business plan to train throughout the year, and from March to July run an AAU program. This business model gave me plenty of time at home to focus on other things. The first summer, we played under the name Reaching New Heights, and as you can imagine, that was a lot to put on the jersey of the uniform, and the parents said to get a nickname, since it was tough to cheer for the team saying, "Let's go, Reaching New Heights!" After year one of Reaching New Heights, I begin to desire to put a brand or name on our AAU team, and one day, while driving back with the family from looking at the lights for Christmas, I saw a shooting star flash across the sky. It quickened in my spirit and mind: I should call our new team the Shooting Stars.

So, in 2012, Shooting Stars was revealed. The next summer, we offered tryouts again, and we began to experience growth— we had five teams. Not only did we begin to grow, we began to attract some of the best talent Katy and West Houston had to offer. We started competing for championships, and several players attracted college attention. As we began to experience success, I added a dimension to the business model to use my experience to help our players play in college.

Our 17-U team was pretty talented; we had picked up some very good players, so I started notifying colleges the Shooting Stars had arrived. We had players I felt could play Division One and Two, or NAIA ball. I built a concept of utilizing all the friends and colleagues I had built friendships with over my seven years of college coaching, three years at the Division One level at my alma mater Liberty University, my two years as head coach at Palm Beach Atlantic University, and my two years at Texas A&M International University. Following the second year of our existence, we had college prospects—like Ryan McClurg who played at Texas, Jonathan Mulmore who went to junior college and then on to Georgetown University, Chris Hynes who played at Letourneau University, Chris Buzzell who played at Missouri Baptist—and we had arrived. As the AAU program grew, we also experienced growth in the training program. However, because of unforeseen circumstances, I was told I could no longer train at Faith West. As you can imagine, this was another blow to my ego, psyche, and heart to imagine a place that meant so much to my growth and development, a place where I had cut my teeth in coaching and training, had asked me to leave. It was tough to swallow, but what do you do? You do as the scripture tells us in Philippians 3:14—"I press toward the mark for the prize of the high calling of God in Christ Jesus."

So, I began my training program at Katy Park. It was an open court with six baskets under a covering. I would start training early in the morning eight in the morning to eleven or twelve, before it got too hot, or start at four in the evening and end at seven. Players would come to get their work in and leave; sometimes as many as 20 kids would come through. While it was profitable, it was very taxing on my body, especially my knees, and it was hot. But hey, you do what you got to do, right? Our training program was not just seeing kids get better, but many began to excel to higher levels. This is also where the first concept of my invention took place. As I began to see such progress, I began to think of the possibilities of a training shoe. The following season of AAU, we had seven boys' teams, and I started a girls' team and had two teams. It was another year of growth and expansion. The business was thriving in training and AAU. I also had another layer to the business, discovering the process of creating and inventing a training shoe.

Our third AAU season was met with challenges, because we lost our practice facility, and therefore, we many times practiced outside when we could not rent Katy ISD facilities. After year three and training outside, where we faced inclement weather challenges, and the training season was not so profitable, as we experienced hurricanes and cold winters, so training outside was a challenge. We were experiencing painful growth. I was blessed early on with some wonderful AAU families, many of whom came up with ideas to help resolve many of our challenges. I am grateful to those many families. We got through year three, and many of our players earned the opportunity to play in college. As each year went by, the organization continued to grow. We were getting some of the top players in the Katy area. Throughout this time, God would remain faithful.

However, financial stress and time management became an issue. During the worst time in winter 2013, training was shut down until a faithful parent on one of the teams contacted me about a potential practice and training facility. She mentioned that the church she attended had a gym. She gave me the phone number to the church to speak with the pastor and associate pastor. After a few calls and no response, I thought I would just stop in one day. I stopped in and spoke with a gentleman named Russ Bell, and as God would have it, we had shared past experiences together and knew several of the same people. We were standing in the church gym, and I realized this was the gym Faith West had use for practices and men's league. God had taken me to a place as a reminder of my journey, even when I had experienced the letdown with Faith West. I think God was smiling on me. After a great conversation with Russ, he offered to introduce me to the pastor of the church, Phil Clements. It didn't take long to realize we had a kindred spirit in the Lord. I had a great conversation with two godly men, who not only helped me out, but became friends and mentors. Pastor Phil said, "I feel so good about what you're doing, and my spirit resonates with you. I'm going to give you a key, and I'll talk to the board to get clarity on the usage of the gym." What a mighty God we serve! In the blink of an eye, He comes through. God is faithful throughout all generations. He knows your situation, and He sees your sorrow. Look to Him; He will meet your every need.

Before we knew it, we had 11 teams the following season, and had now become a staple program in the city for young men and women from ages 11 to 18, and several kids were signing to play in college. Our training program grew, since we had a place to belong. Practices were at Katy ISD until the summer, and then we moved over to the church for our summer practices. I built a training program, where we didn't just offer dibbling, shooting, and skill work, but I was also focusing on building the athlete through speed, quickness, agility, and explosiveness in jumping. I continued to explore avenues to create and invent this training shoe. Before we knew it, we had 13 teams, and each summer, we were making strides in winning championships, making it to nationals, and even playing on the biggest stages in tournaments. Many of our players were signing scholarships, and as many as 12 to 15 kids in our program were playing in college. With the continual growth, I had to rent more and more facilities, like the British International School and other sports complexes.

The Shooting Stars had become a household name in the city of Houston, around the state, and even the country, because of top recruits like Kristian Sjolund, who signed with Georgia Tech. Our training program was now training top prospects like Jay Jay Chandler, who plays at Texas A&M, Jamal Bieniemy, who plays at Oklahoma/UTEP, and Jacobi Gordon, who plays at University of California. I know the concept of the Training Boot works, because I have used it to develop top prospects. We have produced other D1 prospects—like CJ Washington, Emmanuel White, Eden Holt, Nygal Russell, Atif Russell, Mikel Beyers, Derek Dickenscheidt, and the list goes on and on. My Reaching New Heights Basketball Program now reaches over two hundred families, as many as 15 AAU Teams in the West Houston and Katy areas through AAU and training. We currently have over 40 kids playing in college, and over 80 have played in college since its existence. God was using everything for His glory. If it wasn't for the redirection of what happen at Texas A&M International University and Faith West, where it pushed me in a different direction, I would not be a successful business owner, trainer, and inventor with a patent. When difficult challenges come your way, don't get bitter—get better. Allow God to lead you and guide you in the direction He wants you to. There is a famous quote that says, "Sometimes, you have to get pushed out, in order to get pushed on," I made this slogan my rally cry. The Shooting Stars is a respectable name in the Houston and Katy area and known for producing top talent and sending kids to college.

27

THE WOUNDED CHILD

One of the challenges I faced was trying to understand who I was and what was I created for through all of the adversity and career changes. On the surface of things, people looked at my life and thought I had it all together, because yes, it was true that I was successful as a high school coach and was successful as a college coach. Yes, I had had a tremendous opportunity for being a part of the NBA agent business. However, people did not know that I was kind of lost and searching for my true calling. As I began to reflect on my journey in my life, it became clear to me why some of the adversity I endured was necessary, but I really didn't know the specifics of who God had made me to be. I identified myself as a coach. But when God is calling you to do something in your life, it usually is much bigger than the title or even the profession. God is calling you to a place where you can you have full understanding of who you are and what you have been blessed and gifted with to impact the people that God placed in your life. For me, I now knew being a trainer and a coach through my basketball and training program was my new path in life. There was a lot of fear that gripped me at the thought of not having a steady paycheck. For the first time in my life, every two weeks or every month, I was not getting a check from a school or university. I was now relying on my own efforts to generate an income to take care of my family. Although I may look confident in my abilities and what I do, know I was terribly afraid inside. You see, being a kid from a broken family in the inner city, growing up with a single mom and six siblings, there was fear and trepidation about money and not being able to pay the bills. This was a huge step of faith for me, one in which I had to put my complete trust in God. I ultimately learned that's what this life is really all about, getting to a place where we completely trust in God, who made us and created us with purpose. As I evolved in this new business adventure, I realized the tough nights and fearful days of not making ends meet came from an empty place in my life. I began to seek God and to dig a little deeper into who I was as a man to find out why I struggled so much with insecurity, doubt, and fear.

It was through my training that I began to use concepts and techniques in training that I found myself wondering if there was a shoe or boot that could give athletes the same effect to help my athletes get quicker, faster, stronger, more agile, more explosive, more balanced, and more flexible. Around the year 2014, I began to discover the possibility of creating a training shoe in which I thought could revolutionize the way people train and rehabilitate. The concepts I was using seem to be working, as many of my athletes in my program began advancing their careers from role players in junior high and high school to becoming stars in high schools and college prospects. Upon my research and discovery, there was not a shoe like that at the time. So, I embarked on a new journey in inventing my own training shoe. As a former student athlete and coach at Liberty University, I would get emails from them. One late night, I was up and saw that they were launching their own new School of Engineering. It occurred to me in that moment, I wonder if they could help me create a model or prototype of my training shoe. In 2016, I went back to my alma mater and met with the School engineering department Capstone Projects to create a digital prototype to get me started on my new project.

On my way back to Liberty, I remembered how much I love to drive. I believe those are times and moments where I get to reflect on my life and have my God time. I drove to Liberty University as a college student, and here I was in 2016, driving back for a totally different agenda. While I was driving, I was in North Carolina, getting ready to cross into Virginia when a song came on— "You're a good, good father. That's who you are, that's who you are." That song brought me to tears, and all of a sudden, I felt like there was a voice speaking to me, telling me, "You once travelled these roads, seeking your purpose in life, and now you're traveling this road to live out your purpose."

I know many of you can't imagine me crying like a baby, but that's exactly what happened as I rolled into the state of Virginia and overwhelming feelings of everything that I had gone through that had brought me to this place. I had an unbelievable visit at Liberty. They accepted my project into their capstone projects, where the engineering students take on an outside project for their semester. I had a wonderful group of young people who were very eager and worked very hard to help me create what I now call the Edge Athletic and Rehabilitation Shoe. I'm so thankful for Liberty University, but more so thankful for those young people who helped me feel the goal of creating a training and rehabilitation shoe. Upon my returning home, I was overwhelmed with such joy and fulfillment in my heart.

As I made my way home to Houston driving from Virginia, I begin to do more reflection on who I am, where I came from and this vision of this little boy who was sitting in the corner in the room with his other siblings as his biological father came into the house, being very abusive and yelling at his mom, and yelling at the kids for crying. This vision of this little boy with his head between his legs and hands over his head was a picture of what God was showing me where all my hurt, fear, and rejection had begun. I began to sob and weep as I continued down the road, feeling like God had revealed something in me that has been holding me back all those years. On the outside of all of the accomplishments and things I was able to achieve, in some ways, I was still the scared little boy sitting in the corner. As I was launching this new adventure of being an inventor, as well as a businessman, a trainer, an entrepreneur, and of course, a coach, I begin to realize whenever I faced challenges and adversity—whether in my relationships or in my profession—this wounded little boy had been in my subconscious all along. This new journey I was on in my personal life became about healing me from my past as much as it was preparing me for my future. God had begun to do a work in me I had never known existed in 47 years.

You see, many people who grew up in abusive homes have an awareness that haunts them their whole life. What I began to realize was that I was not aware that this child in me ever existed, that it was always masked in my accomplishments and my success, and at this stage in my life, where I find myself alone, I had to deal with this child. As I continued on my way back, the very presence of God came into my car and comforted me, gave me great peace, and began to impart knowledge and understanding in my heart in life about just who I was. I began to learn that although the Johnson family loved me unconditionally, supported me, encouraged me, and had built me up and given me structure and discipline, I was now being given a new task to allow God to heal me from that wounded child.

The exciting thing for me was I realize the process had begun of my new project in creating and inventing a training and rehabilitation shoe. I returned home, where I began working on more research and development of techniques and concepts to bring this training shoe to fruition. There were regular conversations and emails between myself and the capstone group from Liberty, in which we discussed any hiccups that might prevent the project from happening. The spring of 2017 rolled around, and the students had completed the project and were presenting it as a final grade for the semester. I was invited back to Liberty to see the project in completion and to watch the presentation. It was a tremendous sight to see what those students had come up with, and I was humbled by the fact that this kid was on his way to creating something special.

One of the wonderful things about returning to Liberty to collect the project was I was accompanied by one of my brothers, Johnny Leary, and my cousin, who is like my sister—Jackie Coleman—who drove with me to Liberty to make sure I wasn't too tired to drive up to like the project and drive back, because I was in the middle of my basketball season. It was great to have them on the trip, as I got to show them the place where I had grown up, found God, and found my purpose— the place that had completely changed my life from what we had known as kids.

28

I AM AN INVENTOR, BUSINESS ENTREPRENEUR, A TRAINER, AND A COACH

Now that I had some semblance of what I was trying to create, I needed a patent lawyer to help me get a patent for my creation or invention. Once again, I turned to my adopted parents to hook me up with the patent lawyer he had used in getting a patent on some things he had discovered in the oil industry. Pops took me to meet with Charles Knobloch. I explained to him my idea of what I was trying to get done, and Charles took on my project. It was a long and grueling process to get a patent for a new discovery of this kind, because it was a combination of things that already existed. However, Charles was very diligent and determined to find a way to get me the patent. Something I am totally indebted to him and grateful to him for all the work he did for me. I consider him a true friend. There were times throughout the process in which I didn't know whether I was going to be able to get the patent. When Charles came back with our first-round response from the evaluator, there were at least ten previous inventions that conflicted with mine. Now, the goal was for me, as the inventor, to find a way to word things, so they did not conflict with other inventions. With the help of Charles and my dad, we, little bit by little bit, began to avoid several of the conflicts. However, there were still questions by the evaluator on whether or not this could actually be an isolated product. So, the meeting continued as well as further research continued to find more appropriate wording for the perfect presentation to get the patent. Not sure if you are aware of what it takes to get a patent, but there is a timeline in which you need to submit the information to the evaluator within one year to be granted the patent free and clear. We got to a crossroads: we needed to reword some things, but we were not quite sure just how to go about wording things in order to avoid the other invention. So, Charles had the idea that we call the evaluator and ask him what is it that he's looking for? Charles also invited a young man in, who he thought was sharp and maybe could add some value to wording the patent. We called the evaluator, and he was gracious enough to get on the phone with us and answer all the questions we had. By the time we got off the phone, Charles felt like we were going to be granted the patent. The evaluator commented that he was being so hard on us, so we could have a patent that would be free and clear and could not be copied. That statement was music to Charles's ears. However, it was time to get back to work and write up the things he was wanting. There was a time when I had had so much trust and reliance on Pops that he only had to go to Mexico for work and therefore, he was going to miss the meeting in which we were going to pull everything together. I called him and asked could he be there, and he told me, "Steph, you really don't need me. This is your invention. You have all the knowledge that you need, you just need to believe in what you are presenting." Till this day, I don't know if Pops knows how much that meant to me, because I was that scared little boy calling him, not believing I was capable of writing the necessary things to be granted the patent. But I stayed up all night one night and wrote things down. As I met with Charles the next morning, he told me, "This is everything that I needed. I'm going to put all of this information together, and we are going to present it." So, that's exactly what Charles did.

One of the most valuable lessons you can learn in this life is to believe that you are enough. I once heard Pastor T.D. Jakes say, "David believed he was enough to slay the giant Goliath, and he used what he had and what he was use to using just slay the giant". You see, we are gifted in so many ways yet we allow our fears and failures, and pastinsecurities to dictate what we think the outcome will be instead of believing we are good enough and using the talents and gifts that God has given us and also using our past experience of victory and achievements and accomplishments to lead us and guide us. David was confident, not because he was David; he was confident because the Scripture tells us that he said "Who is this giant from Philistine? If I killed bears and lions, why should I be afraid of him?" Oftentimes, when we are faced with challenges or new opportunities, we forget about the tools that we gain along the way that prepares us for whatever lies in front of us. I'm thankful for my dad teaching me a valuable lesson, once again: it was my invention, it was my training and experience that brought me to that point. I needed to be reminded that it was within me to be able to do what was necessary to finish the process of getting the patent. "You are enough!"

It was now the waiting game: the time between the evaluator getting all the information and the time where he makes a decision to grant you a patent or not. While we were waiting for an answer, which sometimes can take up to a year or longer, we presented our information in August 2017. I decided I was going to take some time and meet with trainers and others to inquire what they thought of this being a successful product. I was introduced by the alumni department and Liberty University to another alumus by the name of Chip Smith, who runs Chip Smith Performance Lab, where he trains and prepares professional football and basketball players for the draft. Chip lives in Atlanta, so I called Chip to see if I could meet with him and show him what I was working on and get his feedback. Chip was very gracious to set aside some time to meet with me and gave me some positive feedback but encourage me to get the prototypes before he could truly understand what it is that I'm trying to accomplish. On my way back from meeting with Chip Smith, I had another encounter with God, in which I had been continuing to seek him about that wounded child in me. Once again, I was listening to some worship music as I was driving back, and it was as if the Spirit of God came over me once again, and that same vision came into my mind of the little boy sitting in the corner with his head between his legs and his hand over his head. This time in that vision, I saw an extended hand toward me. It was as if God was saying to me it's time for you to get up and move on. This dream like vision of this young wounded child standing up and walking away was a very heartfelt moment. I realize God loves me and had a greater purpose for me, He saw my heart, my cry, my fears, my failures, my disappointments, and my deepest inner pain. I realize this image of a hurt abandoned child sitting in this corner and a hand extended to him was me. It was as if God had reached down and pulled me up and I got up and walked away. I can't explain to you what this amazing feeling of peace that came over me. I felt in that moment God had stepped out of Heaven and came down to pick me up and free me from that wounded, neglected, abused child that I have lived with all these years. Although difficult times still come my way and it's difficult at times to process, I'm not that same fearful child, I know deep down inside that God has a purpose for the pain. As the months went by September, October, November, and into December, we had not heard anything from the U.S. patent office or from the evaluator. So, I jumped back into my business at hand, which was being a trainer and a coach. During the high school basketball season, I often go out and see the players in my organization play, and it was one particular Friday night I was at Katy high school basketball game when I received an email from Charles saying, "Merry Christmas, you have been granted your patent". Sitting at the game all alone, I couldn't help but smile and jump for joy and the inside that God took a wounded child full of pain, neglect, fear, and doubt and took me on a journey to where now I can say, "I am an inventor." I immediately sent a group text to my family members that I had been granted the patent rights to the athletic training and rehabilitation boot—what an awesome God.

I can now be googled as an inventor with a number, and it's not a driver's license number or jail house number with the crowning achievement of the United States recognizing an idea and granting a patent. Patent Number US9937374B2 will forever be in the history books of a patent given to Stephone Leary, a kid who had no educational foundation, no structural foundation, who accomplished something this great. Now that I am an inventor, I have grown an appreciation for those who have been through that process. I even reflect back on history and how history tells us there were many inventions created by black men and women who were never granted patents because of slavery or the inability to financially process the product. I'm eternally grateful and proud to call myself an inventor. The journey continues now to making this product a reality that hopefully, one day, will revolutionize the way people train and rehabilitate. It gives me great hope that one day this product will change the life of individuals who could not perform, walk, or demonstrate any dexterity movement. I hope and pray this product will help people begin to walk and perform at high levels.

It doesn't matter what your situation is, where you start, or even the bumps and bruises along the way, the ups, the downs, the twists and turns—God has a purpose for the pain. It has taken me all these years to realize I wasn't created to live a perfect, pain-free life without adversity. I now know and realize that God uses all of the pain, all of the adversity, and all of the shortcomings, whether it's personal failure or relationships hardships, God can still use you. I don't harbor any ill will toward my biological father, Willie Leary. I forgive him. Nor do I resent growing up in a single-parent home with my mom, Gladys Coleman, with seven kids in a two-bedroom apartment, nor do I harbor resentment toward my failed relationships, nor even the people in my jobs that made my career as a high school and college coach short-lived—I forgive them. This journey has been about me discovering and finding out who I am, who I was made to be, and knowing that there is a God who loves me and wants nothing but the best for me, even through the most difficult times. I would've never imagined in a million years that Stephone Leary would be the inventor of "The Edge" Athletic Training and Rehabilitation Shoe. An independent business owner, with 13 AAU teams, producing some of the top players in the Katy area and top prospects for college. A top trainer in the community who created innovative concepts to help develop young men and women. An entrepreneur who is looking to grow a brand and build a community and training complex. An author of *They Call Me Coach*. I never even imagined being a coach of a high school football state championship, girls basketball state championship, boys state championship baseball state playoffs NCAA division 1 March Madness and Coach 2 NCAA Division II schools. They call me Coach, because that's the journey I traveled, but coaching is what I did; it's not who I am. Coaching chose me, and I am proud to have all the experiences it taught me. I'm just a man who, like everyone else, was born into a tough situation, who had overcome obstacles and challenges in their life. I'm just a man who is striving to be the man God is calling me to be, and to fulfill His purpose in my life. I've been blessed, because I'm a black man who was raised in a white home in a suburban community with a family who embraced me loved me and accepted me for who I was, who taught me Godly principles and guidelines, who gave me educational structure, and discipline. They introduced me to a loving God, taught me how to worship Him and live for Him. I'm proud to be able to be a bridge and an understanding for other people to know and realize that God can use anyone to change your path and your life to accomplish the purpose he has for your life, whether they're white, black, brown, or whatever ethnic group God can do amazing things when we love and accept each other for who we all are in Him. I'm excited about the next phase of now getting prototypes to demonstrate the possibility of this Athletic Training and Rehabilitation Shoe to revolutionize the way people train and rehabilitate. I hope that someday this product will help people, through the grace of God, walk again.

I want to thank all those who have played a pivotal role in helping me be the man that I am today. I also want to thank all the players and families who have been a part of my journey in being a coach and trainer. I could not be who I am without you. I encourage each and every one of you who have the opportunity to read this book to first know and understand that Stephone Leary was not perfect; he didn't do everything right. I don't want you to feel sorry for me, for my life has been great, regardless of my shortcomings, my failures, and my accomplishments. I'm blessed beyond my own imagination. I encourage you to live out your dreams. Don't allow the pain of your past, the wounded child in you, the hurt from a parent or a teacher or coach or friend— don't allow that to keep you from allowing God to pick you up, deliver you, and help you walk away from that which holds you back. Always have faith over fear, belief over doubt, and love over hate. We all can be a part of making a difference in this world. We've all been given talents and gifts to use, not only for our own crowning moments of achievements, but also to impact the world around us, the community we live in, and to affect and influence the people around us. Let's all commit to being that which God has called all of us to be. Peace, love, and encouragement to you all.

29

INVENTOR "WHO ME"

Many philosophers and inventors say there are three keys to a successful invention:

1. Solve a problem.

2. Make it manufacturable.

3. Tell a great story.

4. Has value in the industry, or life-changing for society.

This chapter has been inspired by the realization that anyone can become an inventor if they're willing to use their creative mind to take them to a place where the imagination flows. Many people have a great story to tell. The key to being an inventor is to open your mind and not limit yourself to the possibilities of the very things that we see and use in our everyday life. I was once told to never try to reinvent the wheel, just try to keep it going and make it better. I took those thoughts to heart and started to see things in a different light. This is an inspiring story of a young African American man who never knew quite how he was educated, who had no structural foundation while he was young, but still found himself to be a pretty good student once his environment and structure changed.

Throughout all the challenges I faced in my life, this young man, through a path of sports and training, discovered a technique and concepts that once put together, could possibly revolutionize the way individuals train and rehabilitate. As far as I can remember since I was that young man living in the inner city, we always looked for ways to become faster or quicker. In 1986, my mind began to race in terms of being creative and building. I later discovered that Pistol Pete and his dad, Press Maravich, created ways to help Pistol become quicker with his hands and feet. He used many tactical and unusual ways to build pistol Pete's quickness and hand speed. When I heard these things as a kid, I don't think I quite knew what to do with that information. As I grew older and began to understand the small things that people did to improve their speed, quickness, and jumping ability, it became apparent to me that I was aware of certain things, but didn't quite grasp the full understanding of them. I had seen many basketball and football players wearing ankle weights, and I recall asking some of the older gentleman why they did so, because I wanted to wear them myself.

My brother, Willie Leary, used to work at Target, and I remember he got us some, so we could wear them around and get quicker and be more prepared when we went out to the courts to play basketball. At the time, I really didn't know what I was getting into, just doing what the older guys did to get themselves quicker or more explosive. The things I learned as a young boy stuck with me, even until now. Many techniques and concepts used back then were just that things have become more sophisticated today. My inspiration of being an inventor of the Xxcelerator Training and Rehabilitation Boot stems from my desire to see change and improvement in every athlete I encounter and my deeper desire to help people rehabilitate. I think every player and person has the ability to grow and improve, no matter what the current situation is.

I'm truly humbled by the work and effort that was put into making this product. I would have never thought that I would be an inventor in a million years, but if I can, you can. That's the mentality I think everyone should have. I believe God has placed in each and every one of us the ability to create things. You were created for greatness, you just have to realize what your creativity is. If we can only understand the importance of submitting our gifts and talents to the one who created us, we, too, can be creative. This is the critical piece of understanding who you are, and why you were created the way you were.

30

BEING ME: "AM I GOOD ENOUGH?"

One of the greatest challenges about writing this book was not truly knowing who I was. I know that's hard for many people to believe, because on the outside it looks like I have lived a life that was pretty focused and successful, like it was almost predetermined. However, I think that's the mysterious part of me, which I didn't see it as myself doing what I have done, but God who simply opens doors for me to walk through. As a young man, I committed myself to doing my very best to fulfill God's purpose in my life, but it was a difficult and lonely journey that left me wondering who I was. I had many, many nights of confusion, when I contemplated giving up. From an outsider's perspective, a kid who grows up in the inner city and gets a chance to go out to the suburbs and live in a nice home and get a private school education sounds good, but there are a lot of insecurities that came with that transition. The question you always ask yourself is, "am I good enough?" You see, competing in sports was one thing, but to me, that was second nature, due to the Survival of the Fetus Theory from growing up in the city. When you go to these many different "hoods" to hoop, you had to establish yourself, or you would get bullied—or as we said back in the day, "punked". Also, when you go to the park, there were so many guys there to play, that once you got on the court, you had to win. If you lost and didn't get picked up, you would stand out in the hot sun a long time, waiting for the next opportunity. This really built inside of me a competitive nature that I applied to sports, but I really had no concept or idea of how that correlated to living life. My life was filled with so much unknown, and when the lights came on and I started to see things from a different perspective—although it was a positive experience—there was also this unsure question of was I good enough?

As I have journeyed through life, no matter what challenge I faced in life, in the back of my head, this question has always remained. I finally discovered the power of God in my life and began to understand that greater is He who is in me than he who is in the world. I tried to live my life with that mentality knowing that God had a purpose for my life, and as Philippians 1:6 said, "Being confident of this very thing that he who has begun in you a good work will complete it unto Jesus Christ's day." To some degree, I have lived my life with a healthy fear from one perspective, but an unhealthy fear from another. I was afraid I would not be successful or would not be able to accomplish anything if I ever walked away from God. Scripture says, "The fear of the Lord is the beginning of wisdom." It's a principle I still hold on today. Unfortunately, the unhealthy fear aspect of my life was being afraid of change and being afraid of not being good enough whenever challenges presented themselves. Along my journey of being a successful coach, trainer, business owner, entrepreneur, and inventor, there were always major challenges. Most of them, I had to leave alone. I'm not sure why that always seems to happen, but I choose to believe those were the times when God wanted me to rely only on Him.

I didn't realize until a few years ago that I had lived two different lives. When I experienced difficulties, setbacks, and disappointments, I struggled with finding and believing in my purpose. I believe that once my life changed in 1986, I had lived my adult life as if I had never had a childhood life. I call this my 0 to 17 life—one filled with so many insecurities—and I lived so many years of my life alone, even when I was married. As I explained in the previous chapter, growing up with an abusive father who abandoned us and neglected me, left many scars in my soul that I never realize was there. Throughout my failed relationships and marriage, then later professional failures, I realized that deep down inside, I was a broken man. All those years, I don't think I ever really dealt with my childhood of growing up in poverty, abuse, neglect, and rejection, so when tough times came, I had a hard time just being me and often wondering if I was good enough. I didn't understand. The only thing I was probably convinced of is that I could play the game of basketball well, I could coach the game of basketball well, I could train individuals to become better players well, but I still spent many, many lonely nights questioning and wondering if I was good enough.

I think the success I was able to experience in the many endeavors I embarked upon covered or masked that broken child who had become a broken adult. By far, the most the difficult time in my life has been the past several years. Even though I became an inventor and successful small business owner, I was broken, bruised, and battered emotionally and mentally, and I often found myself not happy with myself— not even able to love myself. The one thing I had was a strong foundation in knowing that God did love me. The one thing I gravitated to when I was first adopted into the Johnson's home was a desire to worship and praise God. I think the seed was planted in me by God, but I believe my mom nurtured that seed, as I listened to her play the piano and sing songs almost daily. I developed a love for praise and worship. Many times, when I gave players a ride to and from games or practices, my radio station was to Christian music. I believe this was the anchor to my soul. It's what I held onto to get through each day and become the anchor I used to get through those many lonely, painful, broken nights. Also, when I came to know Christ, I developed a love for reading the Scriptures or devotions. As I went to bed each night or woke up each morning, my saving grace was listening to Christian music and reading the Word. When I walked outside the door, I felt confident in who I was, not because I had it all together or because I was so talented and knowledgeable— it was simply because Christ in me was my only hope of glory.

It has only been recently that I found myself again. Not to say that it has been easy, because I only just came out of one of the toughest years in my life. Throughout all of my experiences, I only knew one thing to do: just believe in God and know He has a purpose. I was at a time and place in my life when all of the accolades of being a high school and college star were gone, even my early years of coaching successes were gone, and I was just left to dealing with me. I think the greatest challenge in every person's life was to know and understand themselves and be able to love themselves enough to be the best that God had created them to be. Once we figure this out, we can do our best to learn to love ourselves. Until you become content with the love God has for you and learn to love yourself, you cannot begin to love others, receive love from others, allow family and friends to love you, but most of all, allow God to love you. So, you no longer wake up each day looking for any admiration and applause from anyone or anything, but just taking each day and focusing on being the very best person you can be. Allow God to use you to make a difference by using your talents and gifts to impact this world.

That has been my challenge recently, just loving myself and being me, and that has to be good enough for everyone else. Even in the darkest moments and toughest days, you have to know and believe that God loves you. You have to walk in forgiveness and love toward all those who perceivably hurt you or were a part of your failures and disappointments. That is one of the keys to allowing God to love you, as well as forgiveness. To experience this love fully, you have to love and forgive. There's a cycle that permeates from generation to generation. These two things are critical in breaking the curse, or breaking the chains that hold you captive from becoming the best God created you to be. I know this can be very difficult. I had to come face-to-face with the broken and abused child in me, who didn't know how to handle rejection or disappointments and caused me to live with some fears. The enemy desires to use your past hurts to hold you captive, to paralyze us, and to keep us from experiencing the freedom of God we need to experience the greatness of God. There are seeds of greatness He has placed inside of us. Although there are many tearful nights involved in the process of healing, accepting, believing in yourself, and having faith in God that you were created for greatness, I truly believe your tearful nights will have a joyful morning if you just keep the faith. I have learned that changing zip codes doesn't define you or exclude you from hardship or keep you from having to deal with the broken foundation that so many of us grew up in.

I learned that God is a faithful God, and He loves us so much that he desires to make us whole and complete, and to experience the blessings He has in store for us. But with so many of us, we have to go back and heal from the brokenness from our childhood. There are so many things that are directly connected to the failures and disappointments in our current day-to-day life that are a direct reflection of our childhood traumas. Many of us were given a cracked foundation, therefore, the house we built was shaky. God has shown me so many things through my personal relationships, my business drive, my professional ups and downs, and even through this process of becoming an inventor and writing this book. You can't imagine how difficult it has been to go back and relive some of the pain of my past— the hurt and disappointment. But I believe it's necessary, because that's where the healing comes from when we gain a new perspective of the faithfulness of God. If I can, you can, so you are good enough and can do this!

31

UNEXPECTED CHALLENGES

Oftentimes, we find ourselves moving right along in life, and everything seems to be going well. Then, all of a sudden, tragedy strikes and adversity happens, and a storm of life causes you to drift or spin to a place in life where it seems like everything you thought and dreamed of accomplishing is in jeopardy. This situation happens in everybody's life who aspired to do great things. Sometimes, the challenges in our lives, God put there for us to change courses, or for us to be changed on the course. I'd like to think of myself as a spiritual man. I've read the Bible many times and love a lot of stories in the Bible— particularly the story of Jonah finding himself in the belly of a big fish. Sometimes, we get comfortable in doing the things we love to do and enjoying life as we know it. I don't think any successful person or inventor will ever know the path and course they need when they sit down and think. When you're going through the phase of inventing, there's so much unknown, simply because you're relying on your patent lawyer, on a pad in process, a patent evaluator, and most of all, the patent board of the government of the United States of America to approve a product that only you fully comprehend what it does. Somehow, those unexpected challenges find their way into your life. In my case, I was just coming out of two major transitions in my life when I began this process.

As a man, the most important thing to you is your career and your family. For me, both of those things were challenged in unexpected ways. I had been coaching and training for 20 years before I got the idea to invent this training boot. After 20 years of coaching and training, I was in the midst of a new marriage and a change of course in my professional life. I was in this major shift from coaching college basketball and taking a stab at the NBA Agent Business and Training to going back to high school coaching and starting my own training and AAU program.

32

A YEAR OF SETBACKS, ACCIDENTS, AND SCAM

I'm so grateful and thankful I am sitting here and able to write this book that hopefully will inspire others who may have traveled a similar path. Whereby, on most accounts seems to be a productive successful life, but with many, many trials and challenges. I'm thankful to be alive and able to do what God has put before me to do.

It all began in July 2018. I was traveling to San Antonio to an AAU tournament with my girls, and I was driving behind an 18-wheeler, where I noticed something was loose on the truck. Trying to be very cautious, I decided I was going to drive around the truck, only to have a cinderblock come flying off the truck into my lane while I was traveling 80 miles an hour. As I saw the cinderblock getting ready to hit my car, I hit the brakes, only to have it hit the ground and bounce up and down underneath my car causing a gas leak, oil leak, and a busted radiator, causing my car to shut down. We were in somewhat of a dangerous situation, because cars were driving fast in both lanes, trying to avoid the cinderblock that was now bouncing up and down the freeway. I finally got an opening to veer to the right and make it to the side of the road. It was a very frightening moment, but God and his angels protected me from any harm.

I have always been somewhat aware, but I have a special calling on my life, therefore, whenever tough times arose, I always stopped the enemy from keeping me from doing that which God wanted me to do. So, I was able to move forward. However, February 2019 came around. I had rented a car from Enterprise on a Friday evening. I had attended a high school basketball playoff game. On my way home, I took the back road. It was raining a little bit, and as I was approaching a curve, I hit the breaks, only to realize they were not stopping me. I began to panic for a moment, because it was a dark road, and I could not see what was ahead of me. As I continued to get closer to the turn, I realized after hitting the brakes several times, the car was not going to stop, so I had a choice to either hard to turn the car and turn it over, or keep going straight and see where I landed. I chose to keep the car straight, and before I knew it, I had jumped a ditch and rolled into a brush of weeds and trees. I was shaken up pretty bad, but I did not hit a tree. The bouncing up and down in the car shook me up, hurting my shoulder, my back, and my knees. Once again, I realized God must have a purpose and a plan for my life, because although I was hurt, I was still alive and well enough to continue doing what I do.

I had registration for my AAU basketball season in the next few days, I told myself the show must go on and limped into the meeting to get the AAU season started. I was pretty banged up for a couple months before I felt somewhat normal, and in July 2019, I thought I had made it through the season and could now rest—only to find myself in another car accident in Dallas. It was the very last day of the AAU season, and I was driving back from Dallas. It was raining, and I came around a curve where a truck was sitting in the lane, trying to make an improper turn. I hit the brakes, and this time, the brakes did work. However, I slid right into the back of the truck. It knocked me out for a brief moment, and I found myself in the ditch to the right. The smoke that was inside of my car woke me up in a panic, and I was trying to get out of the car, but all the doors were jammed and locked. While I was coughing, I used my strength to push a crack in the door with my legs and my arms enough to squeeze out of the truck. It was a very frightening moment. Then, I sat on the ground in the rain, just broken and confused, here I was in another car accident.

I called my mom in tears, asking why this was happening to me over and over again. At this point, I found it hard to find some solace in knowing that God loved me or had a purpose for me. At this point, I was discouraged. Not knowing and understanding that this had nothing to do with God, but an enemy who desires to distill to kill and destroy. There's nothing he would want more than for me to be discouraged, to give up, to quit, to question God, to lose faith or hope in God. I have seen the faithfulness of God so much, even this could not make me question God, so I questioned myself. I said to myself, "What am I doing that is causing all of this to happen to me?" I have learned we sometimes need to ask ourselves the question, "What are we doing so right that the enemy of our souls would want to keep you from doing what you are doing?"

Fortunately, I was not hurt too badly, but I was banged up again. When you're going through such challenging and difficult times like these, it's very easy to question God. It's very easy to get discouraged, to give up, to quit. But it's in these times that you find out just what you're made of, and to be honest, you find out whether or not you are built for this. This was probably the beginning of the time in my life when I needed to look a little bit deeper inside of me. When you're on the path to doing great things and making a difference in the life of people along the way, you will encounter adversity and challenges of all kinds. Mine just came in the form of car accidents, physical bleeding, emotional attacks on myself, and spiritually challenging my faith. When you have nothing else to do, because you can't walk, or are barely moving around, you find yourself in a position to read and write a lot. I decided I was going to use this time to finish my book to open my heart and my eyes to understanding how God was making a shift in my life.

I attended a workshop in Phoenix, Arizona in September 2019, and I truly believe this shift was in place all of this adversity I was facing was to prepare me for my next step in my journey. I showed up to this joint venture summit on Just Like God. There was a man there, Jeff, who had no legs and no arms. He was one of the guest speakers. The first night I got there, Jeff spoke about his testimony of him going through some difficult stuff growing up in foster care, no one loving him, and no one wanting to be a part of his life. But God was using him in a miraculous way, giving him a platform to travel around the world and share his testimony.

As he was speaking, tears welled up in my eyes, reminding me of my journey the time and place where I had met God. I felt a peace and comfort of knowing God had His hand on my life, even as I sat there in Phoenix, Arizona. This was very comforting and very timely for me. I was battling thoughts and being challenged in my faith. I returned from Phoenix with a renewed spirit, mind, soul, and body, and I was looking forward to the shift that God would place in my life. However, as I pursued the many ventures I had on my plate at the time— trying to launch and sell my shoe, finishing my book, and beginning to think about launching a speaking campaign—I was also thinking about the possibility of leasing a building, so my business would have a home and not have to deal with the adversity we had faced the year before at my AAU and training program. I had a lot of things I was juggling.

The one thing I learned from the summit joint venture was that I needed to join social media, and use Instagram and Facebook to announce to people that my book was coming soon, my shoe was going well, and my availability to speak. For the first time in my life, I joined Facebook and Instagram. Just when I thought I was making progress in December 2019, I received some threatening messages in my Twitter and Facebook about sending someone in Africa $10,000 or they would ruin my life.

Not really thinking this was serious, I actually asked the person why they needed the money, and they said it was for someone in their family who was sick. I told them if I had it and you asked me for it, I would probably give it to you, but threatening to ruin my life was not going to make me send them the money. So, one morning, I woke up, and one of my AAU Coaches asked me If I had seen my Twitter account. I responded that I hadn't, and he said there were some inappropriate pictures on my Twitter page. I immediately realized the person out of Africa had been real. I immediately did whatever I could to shut down my account and even contacted a very good friend—Clark Dickenscheidt, a private investigator—to look into the situation. With his help, we were able to get the account removed, but there were people who saw the inappropriate pictures.

After three accidents and this scam, I had just about had it, and for the first time in my life, I questioned whether God even loved me. After everything I had been through in my life, I finally arrived at a point where I did not understand what God was doing. I was hurt, crushed, and close to being defeated. The main thing was I was tired. After my body had been bruised and beaten up from the car accidents, I was dealing with a financial hit and a scam. I really felt like I had hit rock bottom. Sometimes, when we experience and go through the most devastating times in our lives, God is reaching a little bit deeper to cleanse us, to heal you in order to take you to another level. There were many nights and days where I found myself questioning God, but every day, I tried to continue to make positive steps to reading devotions and the Bible and praising Him through one of the most difficult situations I had faced. Through many dark days and nights, God showed himself to be faithful. He began to bring understanding in my life.

I lived my life trying to outlive ages 0 to 17, and embrace ages 17 to 50, but I learned that God grows us through things in our life, so He can take us back to the place and show us his faithfulness throughout our whole life. For the first time in my life, I had to come face-to-face with Stephon Leary, who had grown up in poverty, who was broken and beaten up, who was now facing his own shame, failure, fear, and doubt. The question was: what was I going to do about it?

Although it's been a tough stretch in my journey, the one thing I know is God is faithful, loves me, and has a purpose for me. Even in my darkest days and my greatest challenges, my God supplies all my needs. I encourage you to look to Him no matter what the situation is, because no matter what the challenges in my life were, God was faithful. He cares about your situation. God is going to use every single circumstance in your life to grow you, to mature you into being the person he created you to be, so you may accomplish great and mighty things. I can't explain everything about God, nor can I understand all the things of God, but the one thing I do know is that He is a loving and faithful God. You can trust him, you can lean on Him, and in your most desperate times, He will see you through. Even though I have not completely come out of the setbacks I have had over the past year or so, I know God is faithful, and He has a plan. He is a redeemer and restorer of all things, and I know He's able to do great and mighty things. So, I encourage you, as I encouraged myself, to trust in Him. He is the author and finisher of our faith; He is the Alpha and Omega, the beginning and the end. He is God and God alone.

33

GET OFF THE BENCH AND GET IN THE GAME

This chapter is dedicated to those who find themselves in a struggle in this game called life. As a coach of 28 years, I have always told my players that the game of basketball is a beautiful game that teaches us many valuable lessons and develops our character, because they both come with rules, regulations, guidelines, stipulations, and requirements to be the best you're capable of being and to be successful at it. Pistol Pete Maravich taught me a valuable lesson that holds true to me today— lesson of character that goes beyond this great game of basketball. It's the character of life, which is necessary to experience the greatness of achievement and success. You see, as a basketball player, I was taught to act tough, dominate, talk trash, and embarrass your opponents, and if they weren't on your level, let them know. This was a very bad attitude; you have heard the saying, "your attitude will determine your altitude."

I was always a pretty good athlete. I played four varsity sports: football, baseball, basketball, and track. Never was I ever told my attitude or character was important for me to be successful or great. This lesson changed the course of my life. So, I ask you, why do you think you're on the bench? What's keeping you on the bench in this game of life or in the sports you enjoy playing?

You must see yourself the way God sees you and know that He has a purpose and plan for your life. Here's what the Scripture tells us:

"For I know the thoughts that I think toward you, saith the Lord, thoughts of peace, and not of evil, to give you an expected end." –Jeremiah 29:11 KJV

Many of us quit, stop, or refuse to go further, because we don't respect the process of starting small. It doesn't matter where you are, you can always begin somewhere to get to where you want to go. This is the beauty of a success process: enjoy where you are and embrace the journey. You have to have an attitude that it's okay to start small but continue to envision the greatness that lies ahead. Find the passion and joy of pursuing greatness and success, and never ever, ever lose hope. I nearly made the worst decision I could have made when Pistol Pete told me I didn't deserve the MVP award. You can't imagine how I felt in that moment. I nearly quit, because I had finally heard the truth about what was holding me back or keeping me on the bench in my life. It was my character, the kind of character that prevents opportunities to become great or successful. But after some encouraging words from Coach Dave Stallman, I realized there was more to life than just being great at basketball or humiliating your opponents.

My life was changed forever. So much so, I use the phrase "Building Character Through Athletics" for my Reaching New Heights/Shooting Stars Program and my high school and college coaching. Not to mention my eyes were open to all the possibilities that God had for me when I became a Christian. A foundation was laid to now build a new life and new perspective on. I believe that until we come face to face with our own inhabitants that puts us on the bench, we will never fulfill our fullest potential in anything and become great or successful. This makes me think about the coaches, teachers, parents, mentors, and leaders in your life. Has anyone tried to point out the things that may have be keeping you on the bench? Until you embrace those shortcomings and are willing to deal with them, you cannot move forward. You will always be stuck in a rut and looking for something or someone to blame for not succeeding the way you always desired. That is a great place to start. Many of you need a different perspective, and many of you may need a fresh outlook on life. In my experience, the only and best way to fulfill your life is to be filled fully by the one who created you. I found that Jesus is the way the truth and the light! I encourage you, if you are a Christian, to get off the bench and allow God to do a work in and through you. Rediscover your hope, your dreams, and your passions. It is Christ in you that is the hope of Glory. In you don't consider yourself a Christian and look for a peace, a love, and a purpose— as I was as a 17-year-old kid at a basketball camp—I encourage you to simply say these words, "God, I realize I'm a sinner. I realize you are God and God alone. There is no other God before you. I thank you that you sent your only begotten son to this earth to die for me and my sins. Right now, in the name of Jesus, I ask you to come into my heart and be my savior. I pray this in Jesus' name. Amen."

I am so excited for you if you prayed this prayer. You now are called a Christian—a Christ believer. I pray that God will instantly open your eyes and enlighten your life and perspective. You now understand that in "For God hath not given us the spirit of fear; but of power, and of love, and of a sound mind." –2 Timothy 1:7

Go love yourself and love others, use the power you been given, and believe, "I can do all things through Christ which strengthens me." – Philippians 4:13 KJV.

Lastly, go be wise, gain knowledge, and have a sound mind in all your decisions. This new journey and walk with God is a faith journey. Scripture tells us, "Now faith is the substance of things hoped for, the evidence of things not seen." –Hebrews 11:1. When you don't see God in the midst of your struggle, know He's always there, He promises to never leave us or forsake us. Keep your faith in every situation. And finally, Scripture tells us on four occasions in James chapter two: "For as the body without the spirit is dead, so faith without works is dead also." As you maintain your faith throughout your journey, understand there is work to be done. You cannot sit idly by and think things will change, or your situation will get better without understanding that you will have to work for what you want. "And whatsoever ye do, do it heartily, as to the Lord, and not unto men." –Colossians 3:23 Enjoy the journey, there will be good days and bad days, ups and downs, twists and turns, pains, defeats, setbacks, and betrayals— as was evident in my journey. However, through it all, know God is preparing you for greatness. Challenges are not there to define you; they are there to shape you and mold you into who God wants you to be. "Above all, Trust in the Lord with all your heart. Lean not to your own understanding; in all your ways, acknowledge Him, and He will make your paths straight." – Proverbs 3:5-6

Now, let's dive into those questions of bench players. Coach, why am I not in the game? Having coached and trained thousands of athletes, there is one constant theme: no one likes sitting on the bench. As I was writing this book, I began to wonder why we accept being a bench warmer in life. The greatness you will achieve is already deep inside of you. Once you know who you are and where you are in your process as I explained earlier, it's time to wake up to the reality: what is it that's holding me back? I surmise that many of us are not aware of what's holding us back. So, I want to share some things for you to have a self-evaluation of why you might be a benchwarmer in your sports activities and life.

Let's start with the infamous word: attitude. You will find GREATNESS when you accept and conquer SMALLNESS!

Many people get discouraged because they refuse to start small. The Scripture tells us: "If you are faithful over a few things, God will make you a ruler over many."—Matthew 25:21

Who ever said the bench was a bad place to start? It's the wrong mentality to see the bench as a bad place to start. For instance, in sports, hundreds tryout, and we celebrate the fact we made the team and are grateful and excited for a new opportunity to pursue our dreams. Yet, we begin to develop an attitude with being on the bench. I would suggest to you that it's a great place to start. Even in business, if you desire to one day work in corporate America, to get into the building at the lowest level of a job that has been offered to you is an opportunity of a great place to start, while working toward ultimately being on the top floor. You have to think about it like this every day: you get to walk into a magnificent corporate building and see both the reality of where you are and where you want to go. You get to see what it takes to get to the top this is an advantage over other people who are driving by the building every day staring and hoping to one day be able to work inside. If you are the server in a restaurant, many people do not have that job. Look at your opportunity to be in the business and have a job as a place to start and learn everything about the business, but one day, you will become the manager or even an owner. As a coach, when a player would come to me to talk about why they are not playing, it was a great opportunity for truth. Sometimes, it's not about your skills, your knowledge, your work ethic, or even your attitude; sometimes, it's just about preparation. I watch players prepare themselves for the moment of opportunity. You cannot force or neglect the preparation process and think you're going to achieve greatness. The great John Wooden said that preparation is the prize. When you learn to prepare properly, you are prepared for any situation. We have to exercise a little bit of patience in the process of becoming successful or becoming great. The biggest mistake players make or people in general make in life is that they do not enjoy or accept where they are on the bench or on the team and begin to develop a negative attitude towards their teammates and the coach. Sometimes, this attitude is not verbal, but in body language.

The first time you get invited to the big board meeting as a businessman is not the opportunity to take over the meeting. It is an opportunity to learn to make yourself aware of your surroundings and to see how you can be a part of a great team. Learn things, so that it prepares you for your opportunity. Just like players on a team, you need to learn to be a great teammate, and great followers become great leaders and achieve greatness. We cannot forget the attitude of gratitude that we had when we made the team or got the job.

What's the bench in your life? Your bed can be your bench, sitting on the couch, watching TV every day, hoping and wishing for an opportunity to come by. When I am laying in the bed depressed, I'm not able to get up and get going. You are where you are, but this great game of life is still going on, so check in the game. You just have to get started, get up, and get going somewhere. Look for small opportunities: small seeds planted become trees, small caterpillars become butterflies. This is a transformation that takes place, as we just do the little things and watch God do great things in our lives. Opportunity will find you when you just keep moving in the right direction. If I can, you can. I'm not special by any means. I still struggle in certain areas that I'm working on to become great. You can do this! The game is going on, the clock is ticking, and opportunities are waiting on you to get off that bench and get in the game.

As I coached, I found that overcoming your fears is another hurdle. We put way too much focus on the results and not the process. Being a results-oriented person and not a believer in process, allows fear of the unknown to overwhelm your thoughts. You began to act on those thoughts with fear –"What if I take a shot and miss?" "What if I try something new and can't do it?" "What if I apply for this job, and I don't get it?" and if you're like me, "What if I try to love again or be loved?" All of these overanalyzing thoughts control your ability to experience greatness in your life. I suggest you instead think, "What if I shoot that shot and make it?" "What if I apply for that job and get it?" "What if I meet the love of my life?" and lastly, "What if I attempt something and succeed?" I have found that we are focusing on the wrong thing, the results. Even if you don't succeed, get up and try again. It's in the trying process that we learn from our mistakes, and we are better prepared for the next opportunity. In everything you do, look to learn from your mistakes and disappointments. I used to challenge all my players to always go through a mental process of learn grow apply it to the next situation. Don't let fear get in the driver's seat of your mind. There will always be fear— even as I wrote this book, I was gripped with fear—but don't let it control you. Let's take a closer look at fear.

The first thing is to understand what fear really is. You may have heard it said that the acronym of fear is

F-false
E-evidence
A-appearing
R-real or

F-face
E-everything
A-and
R-run, or even,

F-face
E-everything
A-and
R-rise.

No matter how you see it, the objective is to realize FEAR only exists in the mind of the one who allows it to. You can't allow your fears to control you, but you can control it. Fear is a word; it does not have the ability to immobilize or paralyze you from doing things. I have found that in order to overcome fear, you must go against whatever the fear is telling you not to do. You will only find out whether things truly exist to prevent you from achieving or experiencing greatness or success. Ultimately, you find that the presence of fear is what tries to keep you from being great, not fear, itself. We have to develop a mindset to push through whenever fear comes our way.

As a coach, there were players who sat on the bench because they were afraid to make a mistake, afraid to take shots. However, I would tell them, unless you go in and try to do the thing, you will never know the result of it. The most gratifying thing is to watch someone check in the game, take a shot, and swish it, because they were prepared to make the shot, but they were just afraid to take shots. You see, it's not until you do the opposite of what the fear is trying to keep you from doing that you will overcome the fear. As a business person, if FEAR is telling you that you can't do that job, I would say attempt to do that job, and overcome the fear anyway. I believe that God wants to do things in our lives that we hold ourselves back from achieving. I'm reminded of Peter in the Bible, when he saw Jesus walking on the water. He said, "Master, if it is truly you, cause me to come out on the water!" Jesus obliged and called him out on the water. As Peter stepped out of the boat into the water, he was overcome with fear. You see, it wasn't that God had not held up his end of the bargain, it was Peter's fear that kept him from being a water walker and achieving greatness. I'd like to admonish people by saying, "Don't ask God to do something you are not willing to step out and do."

The Blame Game is always one of the biggest hindrances from people and players reaching their goals and dreams. I used to tell my players, "You can be the second best or worst, but you can be the VERY BEST YOURSELF." There are two abilities that have nothing to do with skills: ACCOUNTABILITY and RESPONSIBILTY. You must be willing to have honest self-evaluation, and self-reflection before you can be held responsible for your actions. As a coach, employer, or anyone in a position to hire someone or play someone in a game, it is impossible to count on someone who does not want to be held responsible or accountable for their actions. In the same way as an athlete or employee, it's impossible for you to achieve greatness in anything if you are not willing to be coached or taught how to be successful. When observations are made that deserve some attention or improvement, you must be willing to learn, so you can grow. If your coach or boss criticize you, it doesn't mean they don't like you, or don't want what's best for you. It is quite possible it means they care. We can't always respond with "my coach doesn't like me", "my boss doesn't like me", or "my colleagues and teammates don't like me". I would say being liked is part of the success process. No one brags and talks about the guy who comes up short and blames someone else for why they can't be successful. However, we do brag about the person who failed and got back up or was counted out and are now on top. You must receive criticism as a learned critique of a solution that makes you better. It's okay to be told you did something wrong. Would you like to go through life with no one correcting you? All roads lead to a dead end, so you have to be willing to accept instructions to avoid the pitfalls of life.

In the game of basketball, you can't keep going to the place where you're trapped and turnovers occur, because you are going to be corrected and find yourself on the bench. Likewise, in the game of life, you can't keep going to places or doing things that are wrong and expect the law or dangers of life to not cost you your life or put you in jail. Avoid the pitfalls of drugs, alcohol, and illegal activity that the whistle in the game of life hands out as life's consequences. To achieve greatness, you must choose to live a responsible life. Life demands before it rewards. It's going to demand you to do the right thing before you are rewarded anything. Be accountable and responsible, accept corrections, and get off that bench. It's no one else's fault why you are where you are, so take ownership of whatever has happened to you and turn your situation around. If you are willing, God is always willing to bless you on your journey to becoming and achieving greatness.

It is extremely important that as a player or person in life, you avoid being comfortable. You must always remain open to embrace change, to be ready to shift and pivot. Many of us in our lives get to a place where we get comfortable with how we work , with what we do for work, but you should continue to develop a skill and ability to adapt whenever necessary. This is another form of bench warmer: the guy who just does enough to be on the team, but does not embrace what it takes to get in the game. This is the person who refuses to work on other areas of their game, therefore allowing others to pass them up. The challenges that we face oftentimes get exposed by the opponent or challenges that are far greater than ourselves. Therefore, we have to work harder and explore new ideas to better ourselves. The moment you get complacent or lazy, you will allow your challenges or your opponents to overcome you or overtake you. Remember, if the goal is to get in the game of life, you can never be content with just being on the bench. You must push through, work hard, dedicate yourself, discipline on a day-to-day perspective on improving your skills and ability to be effective.

As a coach, I used to tell my players they must train for the world, not just for the school they go to or the community they live in, because I could guarantee there was someone else around the world working very hard to achieve the greatness that you want to achieve. Jobs and positions in sports are very limited, therefore you must prepare yourself to be one of those that a business or a coach can count on when the game is played. There is a point in life where we need to pivot and shift. This is a concept when a basketball player catches the basketball, establishes the pivot foot or permanent foot, from which they cannot move or violate the rules of the game of basketball by traveling. In life, we get comfortable and establish pivot foots, and we don't move any further. In recent training and sports, we use the word shift to describe putting force on the ground and exploding into a direction. I believe that players in the game of basketball can execute skills better when they learn to pivot and shift. I also believe this concept applies to the game of life. When we become complacent in what we are doing, if we truly desire to experience greatness or success on another level, we must pivot and shift in a different direction of opportunity when it comes our way. Shifting is the change that occurs in a person's life that sends them in a different direction than planned. It is also the place of your greatest challenge, the place of your SHIFTING! This is the place where the trajectory of your life is altered, and the place where you are redefined in the eyes of others and yourself. The SHIFTING place may invoke a change of course in your life or profession. This is the place where the prophecy of your life is fulfilled, where the oil of the joy of the Lord is activated. If you are experiencing such a challenge, look out, because things are about SHIFT!

We can't stay where we are and think we're going to get where we're going. Sometimes, the pivot and shifting happens through adversity, when you're exposed, down on your luck, or even from a positive perspective, when you have accomplished all you can in your position, and you desire more. This time requires you to pivot and shift. When you pivot and shift, you never look outside of yourself but look introspectively to see what it is that is in you already, that you had a burning desire to do once before. Muster up the energy in that area and shift. You will see an experience of new opportunities will come your way, and you will be on your way to achieving greatness on another level. Don't be complacent, don't be content and unhappy with where you are. Pivot and shift and explore greatness and success on another level.

One of the biggest reasons why many people never reach their dreams and goals is because they lack the confidence and belief in themselves and have lost hope, therefore causing them to be filled with many insecurities resulting from past failures, rejections, and neglect. Far too many people remain on the bench of life and sports, because they have been mistreated, unloved, abused emotionally or mentally, and told, "you're not good enough", or "you'll never be this or that." I'm here to tell you that you are more than good enough! Greatness is waiting on you to set up and check in the game and believe you can do this! Everything you went through was for a reason. Your greatness is being defined day by day as you overcome your past failures, mistakes, unfortunate heartbreaks, and disappointments. You must understand, no matter what age you are, you are so much further from those painful experiences—it's okay to get up and go on. It's okay for you to try again; it's okay to fail again. It's the failure that's teaching you and preparing you for greatness. After all, the toughest part about sitting on the bench is that it starts to hurt itself. The bench was not meant for a place for you to reside, it was a place for you to begin, to try, to prepare, to work for an opportunity to show the world what you are capable of.

All of these painful experiences should become the motivation for why you work so hard, but you learn to serve to be diligent, to love, and to treat others the way you want to be treated. You were made for greatness! There is a God who created and formed you in your mother's womb. Just think God is the one who desires to do great things in and through you. He's very good at taking broken pieces like you and me and making beautiful things out of it. I am a living testimony. I'm not just a talented man who took advantage of an opportunity to change my life. It's time for you to get off the bench and get in the game. The world needs you, so don't allow or let your past pain insecurity and experiences keep you from impacting the world you live in. With God, all things are possible to them who believe. Never lose your belief in yourself, and the one who Created! Always remember, "For my thoughts are not your thoughts, neither are your ways my ways, saith the Lord. For as the heavens are higher than the earth, so are my ways higher than your ways, and my thoughts than your thoughts," (Isaiah 55:8-9). It may not always seem like God is in your midst, especially when things aren't going well for you. However, know that God loves you! "For I am persuaded, that neither death, nor life, nor angels, nor principalities, nor powers, nor things present, nor things to come, nor height, nor depth, nor any other creature, shall be able to separate us from the love of God, which is in Christ Jesus our Lord" (Romans 8:38-39).

Even in your toughest, most difficult situation as you read this book, please know that God loves. He gave up his son for you.

I personally apologize for anyone who caused you harm or mistreated you to make you think you are not good enough. Take it from me, you are more than enough! Pretend like I'm calling your name to get off that bench and get in the game. Know that I'm cheering for you, wherever you are, and hoping you great success!

34

THE TALE OF TWO CULTURES:
A BLACK AND WHITE EXPERIENCE

I have had the pleasure and unique experience of growing up in two opposing, diverse cultures. My experiences with both cultures have formed and shaped the way I see the world around me. In some aspects, it has given me an insight into what's going on in our nation today with all of the social and racial unrest. Having had the experience of growing up in an oppressive system, I have a different perspective. I believe there are two different ways to look at this. I think we use the word "systematic oppression" to apply to situations that have an inherent system of oppression. What do I mean by that? I believe in the inner city or impoverished community, there is an "inherent system of oppression" and outside of the inner city community, there are "systems of oppression" as they relate to laws, bills, and treatments of black and brown people from the past.

However, I think we can take these two concepts and intertwine them. The message becomes convoluted and combative. As I experienced as a child growing up in the inner-city community of Houston— third Ward, fifth Ward, South Park, Sunnyside, and the southwest side—I witnessed the low-income communities with inherent system challenges of race, education, social classes, and economic classes. But the biggest thing is a system of oppression in the structure of the inner-city family. There is a lack of family structure. Typically, what you see in the inner city is a single mom who works multiple jobs to provide for her family. Oftentimes, even with the multiple jobs, a single mom may need the assistance of welfare. The welfare system has become an inherit system of oppression for inner-city communities. Unfortunately, many families and individuals begin to depend on welfare to make it. Yet, we know, if we want our young kids to grow up to be successful and experience life on higher levels, we must equip them with the opportunities to be successful. Give them a vision of endless possibilities. This dependence on the welfare system creates an excuse that even if someone doesn't get a job, even if they don't get an education, the government will still take care of you. The other form of dependence on the welfare system has become a Social Security check.

I know this is a sensitive topic, because there are people who truly need assistance from the government to give them a boost to provide for the family, while they pursue new opportunities to be able to take care of themselves. The Social Security check was also meant to get a person through until they're able to do other things to provide for themselves and their family. Unfortunately, we see lots of situations where this is not the case. Many individuals and families have become dependent upon the welfare and Social Security assistance. I can remember when food stamps were like money on the street in the hood. The reality is the system was abused by so many people, it started to be used buy drugs and alcohol. These are all things I think are inherent systems of oppression that some of the biggest challenges black and brown, or even white, people who grow up in poverty face. I know, because I was one of them. It wasn't until later in my life that I began to understand the system of oppression as it relates to my mentality, because I had some of those same thoughts that could have kept me from being who I am today, or could have kept me from having the life I have experienced. I believe many missed opportunities happen to our inner-city kids, because we become comfortable with our situation and get stuck in a mentality that doesn't allow for us to envision ourselves as great.

Growing up in poverty in the inner city, do you live with stereotypes and discrimination that affect your belief system? I have had many experiences of mistaken identity, being pulled over by the cops because I was driving a nice car, or even having a conversation with a friend who made bad decisions. Yes, I still panic when cops pull me over, and yes, I live with that guilt by association of being black. I'm proud to say, even today, I have not ever committed a crime. I have never drunk alcohol, nor have I ever done drugs. I believe in the possibility of teaching young people to believe they do not have to subject themselves to live such a lifestyle that would prohibit them from experiencing a life of success. Even though I grew up in a home where alcohol and drugs were prevalent and crimes were committed by some of my siblings, I made the choice to pursue a life of success. My motto is, "if I can, you can." I choose to believe that for every single inner-city, impoverished kid in America and around the world.

You don't know that you are poor until you step outside of your environment or experience another culture that you realize how much you DON'T have. It is easy for us to point out the government or white people for racism or discrimination and overlook the inherent "system of oppression" and the issues black and brown, or even white, people who grow up in inner-city, impoverished communities face on a day-to-day basis. As a kid growing up, my mom told me to be educated.

However, the system in place did not allow everyone to be educated, so it became a choice, and it is a choice that many are choosing not to do. This is the challenge and problem of an inherent system that is being overlooked and simply blamed on white people, the government, or other systematic oppressions.

Many people think that because Stephon Leary moved in with some white people that his life was complete or was good. Little do they know the challenges I was faced with in embracing a totally new culture. It's probably different mindset, because I am definitely a totally different structure. I had many insecurities and little to no educational foundation and structure. Deep down inside, I was excited about the opportunity to play basketball for the new school, but I quickly realized all of the many other challenges I would have to accept and overcome. Yes, this was an opportunity I could not pass up—an opportunity to learn a different culture, and quite frankly, many of those fears and insecurities went away when I realize that the Johnson family loved and accepted me for who I was. I think this concept has been lost in all of this race relations and social unrest conversation. We may have a ways to go in some aspects, but to take broad strokes of racial tension and social unrest on white people is totally unfair. Yes, there are some who are still racist, and yes, there are some systematic oppressions in place that prevent black and brown people from ultimate success in certain industries. However, as I look around today, I'm reminded of when I was a child growing up. Like, "don't go across the track", "you may be killed", or "don't hang out with those white kids, they may beat you up", or "those white people don't like us", or my favorite, "don't date that white girl and have babies with her, because your kid will come out looking different and will not be accepted into society".

People, look around you. We have more interracial marriages and biracial children than we could have ever imagined. Some of our greatest leaders in many professions are biracial, and there are more white families across America who have adopted black children, like myself. We cannot allow for political agendas or racial and social unrest to broaden the stroke of all the positivity that we seen and have experienced as progress in America. We cannot allow the racism of a few police, the racism of those who hold on, to pass teaching, and the unfortunate experiences of mistreatment of black and brown people to keep us from moving forward and accepting and loving one another beyond the color of our skin.

The white culture I grew up in gave me a foundation first as a family structure: I had a curfew. I actually sat down at the dinner table and talked to members of the family about their day or about what was going on in our lives. I would need to sit down or go to a place quietly and do homework before I could do anything else. I was also held accountable for chores around the house, teaching me work ethic and helping each other inside the family. I also experienced praying together as a family, reading the Bible as a family, taking family vacations, learning how to manage money by receiving a small allowance, and I also learned how I needed to get a job to be able to take care of myself and not depend on my family or the government. This was not an easy concept for me to accept. As an athlete who received a full scholarship to college, I did not value working to earn money; I thought I was going to be taken care of. This was a valuable lesson I had to learn. Because I drove cars, I had to put gas in the tank of the car. I didn't realize when it broke down, I probably needed the money to fix it, and I needed to pay insurance. I even had to get over the mentality that I could drive without a license. When I first moved in with the family, I just assumed I could drive without my license, because that's what you do in the hood. This was another learned sensitivity to not breaking the law: get your license first!

As you can imagine, beyond the family structure, I had to adapt to being black in a white society. So yes, I was mistakenly identified. However, it never changed my mind about the family who loved and supported me. We cannot allow the ignorance of the few affect the action and experience of the majority of people who truly love and accept black and brown people for who they are and do desire to give them the best opportunities to be successful. As I grew into a young man, I started to gain favor in the eyes of white people— not just in Katy, Texas, but everywhere I went. I feel like in some sense of the word, I was a living Martin Luther King's "American Dream" as I began to be judged by the content of my character and not by the color of my skin. This love beyond the color of the skin is a great starting point for all to embrace and act upon. Young children don't see or understand our differences, unless they are taught. Unfortunately, the division in America has begun to happen on both sides—black people are stating white people are the problem so much now that white people have to defend themselves and are losing their voice and the desire to help. Even people like the Johnson family, who love beyond the color of one's skin, who lived lives loving and impacting people of all races and all colors, even launching projects of watermill schools and churches in Kenya, are also being judged. We are allowing ourselves to be divided when the actions of a few does not represent the action of the majority of white people like the Johnson family, who just want to love and accept any and everyone who comes their way.

The tale of two cultures has put me in a tough position, where my black constituents think I should think the way black people think, and my white constituents think I should see things their way. However, for me having lived in both cultures, I believe we are allowing the true problem to be lost. It saddens me and breaks my heart to see such violence and outrage over social and racial unrest. I was taught to love beyond the color of the skin, and I know many other people who have experienced this same love.

We need to re-shift our focus back to developing a community and not let racism and discrimination or political agendas divide us in our efforts to cross racial barriers, the laws overstep one another. This is not a race issue: this needs to be torn down by not just the government getting involved, but all those who love and care for people, especially those who need a helping hand. In my opinion, many of our successful athletes, entertainers, businessmen, and entrepreneurs have done a bad job of giving back to the community. We are in a time of social unrest. However, we'd like to look to the past to get the answers, for they are right in front of us— to love beyond the color of the skin and to be willing to invest in creating opportunities for those who grow up in impoverished communities and provide avenues and pathways for them to become successful. That can begin with the family structure, assisting in creating structure in the home and resources to help children of the future. We need to help these educational systems by using our resources to see a program where children can be helped with homework after school and provide extracurricular activities. We have limited the minds of young people in inner-city communities to think in order to be successful, you have to be a professional athlete or entertainer, and when they don't succeed in that, they become directionless. I could not see past being a professional basketball player. My vision for being successful was wrapped up in my limited thinking of what success was.

We have had a black president—who a good majority of white people voted for. In Houston, Texas, we have a black mayor, we have black congressmen and women, and so do other states. We have made tremendous progress in our country. We have to expand the minds of young people to help change the culture of environment infrastructure of the family and educational structure to allow for our kids to dream again. I believe we have shattered the dream of many people in the way the media portrays race relations. We have made tremendous progress in America. Because of sports, entertainment, and business, some of our wealthiest people are black. However, we are allowing a mentality that we cannot be all we are capable of being because of white people or the government. We need to eliminate the excuses and remind our youth, "If I can, you can" and pave a way for the next generation.

I believe this is a tremendous mistake that even our successful black and brown people are communicating. It's not just the systems of oppression that exist in businesses and government in our society that's holding us back, it is also the inherent systems of oppression in our own community. I know for a young black child, like myself, who grew up in a culture where education and success was not prevalent, my mind was limited. However, when my environment and culture I was in changed my life, my experience changed. I began to have a vision of what I could possibly do. We have to help our young people see beyond their surroundings and give them a different look of what success looks like. We can't allow the police brutality of some affect the opportunities that are in front of us, because of racism or discrimination or political agendas. These two cultures and two perspectives about systematic oppression and inherent systems of oppression need to be correctly communicated, so we can change the minds of young people and allow them to dream again.

The cry for equality. What is equality? There can't be equality until there is equal opportunity, but we all have different strengths, weaknesses, talents, and gifts that create opportunities for everyone, and those opportunities presents themselves to all us differently. The question is, are we prepared for the opportunities that are in front of us? Equality doesn't come in a form of envy or jealousy. I know and have experienced many opportunities pass me by, because either I was not ready for change, or had made decisions to not be all in. As a coach, everyone doesn't shoot the same amount of shots. I can remember my former players asking me, "How come they get to shoot or play, and I don't?" My response was always the same, "Have you prepared yourself to do what they do, and when you get the ball, has anyone told you not to shoot? If not, then take the shots and prove you can make them, and you will be empowered and encouraged to continue to do it."

It is not some else's fault we don't take the risk to pursue what we want in life. If you discover what someone else's strengths are that are not your own, DON'T be envious or jealous. Do your best to be the best you. It is teamwork that makes dreamwork. We all can have a role to play in this great game called life. Most importantly, make sure you are prepared for every opportunity that comes your way, mentally, spiritually, physically, emotionally, and skillfully. Usually, what I have learned is there are small dividers in "equal opportunity" that is not race or discrimination-related. Missed opportunities are also great teaching and learning experiences for every individual. Equality means being great at who you are. Sports are a great analogy as to how we interpret "equality". Larry Bird wasn't Magic Johnson and Magic wasn't Bird; they both are doing great, and we are on the way because of the opportunities that were afforded to them. Although one was black, and the other was white, America embraced them both. We can all be great at what we do, but we have to become great in who we are before people accept our greatness. A terrific lesson can be learned from the Magic and Bird experience. Magic Johnson and Larry Bird saw their differences and diversity as an opportunity to show the nation we can love and respect one another and both become great. The friendship that was formed set the stage for America to embrace them both. I submit to you the rise of anger and hate is a spirit of division.

Let's not allow the negative thoughts of a small population control the narrative of racism in America. I believe one of the biggest mistakes that we all are making in an effort to have solidarity and unity among all races is we all think we know the problem and know the answers. We all are operating from limited knowledge, because our true knowledge is based on our experiences. Everything else, we learn from others, their experiences, and what's going on in our society. Sir Francis Bacon is credited with saying that knowledge is power. I agree that knowledge is powerful. But when compared to the power of love, knowledge looks like a weak imitation. Two thousand years ago, a man, renowned for his great knowledge, came face to face with the perfect love, and his life was changed forever. In reflecting on this, he wrote:

"But knowledge puffs up my love build up. Those who think they know something, do not yet know how they act to know. But whoever loves God is known by God."— 1 Corinthians 8:1-3

Like this man, who would end up spreading a message of love to people He had previously despised for their differences, the man who loves God learns to love beyond the color of the skin, because God is love.

The only thing that is constant and does not change is God. He—and He alone—is constant, and His love endures forever!

"Jesus Christ the same yesterday, and today, and forever."—Hebrews 13:8 KJV

I would offer these solutions and long-term strategies:

-Love beyond the color of the skin.

-Help cultivate the infrastructure of the family in low-income communities.

-Educate on freedom and empowerment in the voting process.

-Teach and explain economic empowerment money strategy.

-Rebuild the homes in the inner city or impoverished areas.

-Build community centers with resources outlets.

-Restructure the education process.

-Encourage political empowerment in offices and lobbying.

-Help young people envision themselves in multiple careers.

Let's step a step back from pointing the finger at one another due to race, skin color, political party, or economic status, love one another, and make a commitment to respect, appreciate, and be at peace with all men.

"A new commandment I give unto you, that ye love one another; as I have loved you, that ye also love one another. By this, shall all men know that ye are my disciples, if ye have love one to another."—John 13:34-35 KJV

Lastly, in 1963, Dr. Martin Luther King, Jr. inspired the world with his dream – that one day his children would grow up in an America where they were judged not by the color of their skin, but by the content of their character. I am the fulfillment of that dream. I am the fulfillment of the dreams of hundreds of thousands of white and black Civil War soldiers who gave their lives to end slavery in this country. When they looked down the corridors of time, they saw me. Because of a white coach and a white family, this black man has now become a successful high school and college basketball coach, a trainer, business owner, author, and an inventor with a patent. From the speech in 1963, "The March on Washington", to his last speech in Memphis, he eloquently expressed the progress we have made.

Love changes everything. Acts of love from people of all races toward each other will be the key to healing our nation.

Five years later, in 1968, in Memphis, he gave his last speech before his unfortunate passing. Dr. King spoke of the progress:

"Well, I don't know what will happen now. We've got some difficult days ahead. But it doesn't matter with me now. Because I've been to the mountaintop. And I don't mind. Like anybody, I would like to live a long life. Longevity has its place. But I'm not concerned about that now. I just want to do God's will. And He's allowed me to go up to the mountain. And I've looked over. And I've seen the promised land. I may not get there with you. But I want you to know tonight, that we, as a people, will get to the promised land. And I'm happy, tonight. I'm not worried about anything. I'm not fearing any man. Mine eyes have seen the glory of the coming of the Lord."

Dr. King saw progress in 1968, and so do I in 2020. Sure, there are still some things that need to change as they relate to police brutality and the small percentage of remaining racists or the systems of oppression that still exist. But let us also see the good in each other and the tremendous progress that has come over the many years that will continue to grow as long as we are together as one nation, under God, indivisible with liberty and justice for all.

I Hope

Hope is a wonderful thing, Maybe the best of things,

Hope deferred makes the heart sick and is a tree of life,

Hope never dies!

Therefore, I hope we can look beyond the color of our skin,

I Hope we can love each other the way we all deserve to be,

I hope we can break the chains of generational bondage
that keeps us all from being free to love,

I hope we can learn to live in peace and harmony,

I hope we can push one another

to fulfilling our goals and dreams,

I hope we can cross over from our past way of thinking to
embracing one another with Genuine Sincere Love!

"I Hope" by Stephone Leary

35

MY REDEMPTION STORY

2019 was a very difficult year for me. So many things happened that shipwrecked my faith and caused me to lose hope. I experienced what were the most devastating times of my life. I had experienced difficult times before, but this seemed to be an all-out assault on my life, my faith, my character, and my talent. There were many times I wanted to give up.

At the start of 2020, I began to rebuild little bit by little bit, and I prayed and asked God to begin to restore things in my life. I had to hang on to believing in God to deliver me, and to do what He wanted me to do and to do well, to prosper, and to have hope in the future. I have been running my basketball and training business the past eight years and questioned whether I was even qualified. There were countless days and nights when I questioned just who Stephon Leary even was. The game I loved so much and had given so much to seemed like it was coming to an end. Sports saved my life; without sports, I have no idea what I would have become. I confess whenever something went wrong around me in my relationships, in my job, or in life, my saving grace was always, "go win and conquer something else just to feel good about myself".

As an adult, I found comfort in basketball—whether it was training or coaching. This great game of basketball was and has been good to me, in spite of the achy knees and back from knee surgeries and constant running and jumping for 43 years. But because I did so much in this game, and the game gave so much to me, I couldn't believe I had come to a point where I was contemplating letting it go.

Days went by where basketball became undesirable. Along with the many challenges I faced, one of the difficult things to swallow was the lack of commitment in my organization from a supportive and financial standpoint. Running a business is not very difficult when everyone is all in and committed, because you see a great reward. However, that dissipates, and you struggle to make ends meet and pay your bills and take care of all the employees for their hard work and dedication. I felt like as an organization, we had given so much to the community and helped many people achieve their goals and dreams that people would appreciate you and want to give more for the work you do. This was not the case, and I found myself hurt by that. The Scripture tells us that to everything there is a season. I was going through a season of inexplicable difficulty. When you are going through a season like this, you feel like quitting or giving up, but God is always up to something, even in the midst of your greatest challenges. God is a faithful God, and oftentimes, we fall in love with things that are good for us. God gave us the talent to do well in the gift He's given us. However, He never meant for us to worship the gift, but worship the gift-giver. He is the way, the truth, and the life! Put no thing or God before him. The book of Matthew tells us, "But seek ye first the kingdom of God, and his righteousness; and all these things shall be added unto you."

We get into a place and time in our life where subconsciously, we are on autopilot. God may be the airplane that gets us to our destination, but we start to steer the plane, instead of trusting in Him to get us from point A to point B. We try to navigate a path around storms. Why do we get to a point where we think we know better? He is the author of our faith, the first and the last, the beginning and the end. Why? I suggest we become so good at something, we think we have no need for God. Once again, this is a subconscious thing that plays out in our mind as we rationalize. "Well, I'm doing what God told me to do, it is God who gave me this gift and talent," so we continue on doing things in our own way. But God always has greater plans for you and for me. He desires to take us from glory to glory. Every season is critical in the preparation process to take us to new levels. But for every new level, there is a new devil. So, expect challenges; the good and great things we desire to do, the enemy of your soul does not want you to achieve. As a Christian, you allow God to take you to new levels. Your impact on others will follow, and the enemy does not want to see that happen. We fall prey to the idea that life is supposed to be easy, but this is not case. For every test, God is creating a testimony, so He may use you to do great and mighty things. Will you trust Him? Jesus said, "These things I have spoken unto you, that in me, ye might have peace. In the world, ye shall have tribulation: but be of good cheer; I have overcome the world."

Don't you just love the dichotomy in the Scripture where Jesus declares, "you will have trouble, BUT be of good cheer." No matter what happens in our lives, if we just trust God and His provision for our life, we will overcome whatever challenges we face. There are difficult seasons and yes, even with the things we love the most— our kids, our spouses, our jobs, our friends, and our family. But BE OF GOOD CHEER! I have experienced great depth mentally, emotionally, and physically, been heartbroken many times over, let down, neglected, and rejected on many levels. But God is faithful. With these challenges, I remind you and implore you to be ready to shift with the wind of the direction God is blowing in.

I have been sitting and contemplating this book for a few years, I had a wonderful friend who told me, "Stephon you need to get this book out; people need to hear your story. It's time for you to pivot, shift, and serve God." She was right, not only was this book necessary, but as God would have it, there has been so much healing for me in writing this book. It has been a painful process, many times I got stuck on certain chapters, not having the emotional capability to deal with the pain. I cried many tears on the pages of this book. Redemption doesn't come from how much money we have after we lose it all, or even your business booming after a down year, or finding love after a broken relationship. Redemption is getting back to the place of vulnerability, back to the childlike faith where you trust and believe in God's process. When this happens, and you are ready to shift, He gives you a rebirth experience and vision for the future. He equips you and arms you with whatever you need to take that next step. He opens doors to new possibilities, and that, my friend, is redemption, because you are now on your way to accomplish and achieve great things. I am redeemed, but God says so!

When I say there are many tears on the pages of this book, I want you to know it is okay to shed tears. One of the most powerful scriptures in the Bible is also the shortest scripture in the bible: "Jesus wept." (John 11:35). This scripture occurred when Mary and Martha asked Jesus to heal Lazarus, and he didn't— thus, they were distraught because Lazarus died. However, what's encouraging to know is your greatest moments of being distraught are God's finest hour of restoration and redemption.

As the story goes, Jesus didn't heal Lazarus because they wanted him to, yet he came to them in tears to let them know he cared. Then, he raised Lazarus from the dead. It's important to know things may not happen on your time, but know Jesus cares and will do what He is supposed to do in the moment you need him most. There are many forms of tears. In some ways, tears can be described as one of the complex outward expression of emotions. There are tears of joy, tears of happiness, tears that bring a smile, tears of sadness, tears of discouragement, tears of compassion, tears of devastation, and tears of inspiration and exaltation. I have had the pleasure of experiencing all of these emotions and found myself perplexed by what emotion I was really feeling. This book will hopefully shed some light on this inexplicable emotion call "tears". I hope you discover your greatness in your tears! "They that sow in tears, shall reap in joy."— Psalms 126:5

I pray for you on your journey and encourage you to never lose hope, be diligent and vigilant, stay the course, and keep the faith. "Be strong and of a good courage, fear not, nor be afraid of them: for the Lord thy God, he it is that doth go with thee; he will not fail thee, nor forsake thee." Deuteronomy 31:6 KJV

Love to you all now and forever! "Be careful for nothing; but in everything by prayer and supplication with thanksgiving let your requests be made known unto God. And the peace of God, which passeth all understanding, shall keep your hearts and minds through Christ Jesus."-- Philippians 4:6-7 KJV

No matter what happens in this life, enjoy the journey. Many times, in the Scripture, God changed the name of the people He calls. In Genesis 17:5, "He shall no more be called Abram, his name shall be

called Abraham; a father of many generations have I made thee." In Genesis 32:28, He changed Jacob's name to Israel. Jesus changed the name of Saul to Paul in Acts 13:9. For me, that name was "Coach". It may not have been what I dreamed of doing as a kid, or what I imagined doing while growing up; however, God had a purpose for Stephone Leary, and that purpose would not be fulfilled without the title of Coach. Through all the ups and downs, twist and turns, mountain-high and valley-low experiences, God had a plan for my life, and He has one for you. From the time I got my first job in 1993, until now, they called me Coach. It has been an honor and privilege to have served as a coach, mentor, friend, and father figure to many. They call me Coach!

CPSIA information can be obtained
at www.ICGtesting.com
Printed in the USA
LVHW051129271120
672645LV00005B/559